LE PLAN DE LA VILLE, CITE, VNIVERSITE FAVXBO

S DE PARIS AVEC LA DESCRIPTION DE SON ANTIQVITE

LA RIVIERE DE SEINE

Spiritual Writings
of
Saint Louise de Marillac

Translated from the French by
Sister Louise Sullivan, D.C.

De Paul Provincial House
96 Menands Road
Albany, New York 12204 USA

March 15, 1984

Originally printed May 31, 1983 by the Company of the Daughters of Charity of Saint Vincent de Paul under the title: *Sainte Louise de Marillac: Ecrits Spirituels*

Cover by Sister Joanne Dress, D.C.

PREFACE

The Bible is Jesus Christ: Jesus Christ announced; Jesus Christ revealed; Jesus Christ communicated. The better we know Sacred Scripture, especially the New Testament, the more we will deepen our understanding of Our Savior. By means of this reading and meditation we become filled, little by little, with His personality and with His Spirit.

The same may be said of the saints who are the "friends of God." By revealing to us their experience of God, their writings bring to light their human and supernatural gifts and permit us to follow them on their journey toward God.

Therefore, it is a great grace for us, the Sons and Daughters of Saint Vincent, who have received so many letters and conferences of our Holy Founder, to possess also a large part of the correspondence of Saint Louise de Marillac as well as her diverse spiritual writings. All this constitutes a veritable family treasure.

However, if, in the case of Saint Vincent, this treasure has been and continues to be well used, the same is not true for Saint Louise. It is only very recently that her work has been unearthed from the dust of three centuries. This discovery has already produced a few biographies and studies of great value. It is now a pressing invitation to as many Daughters of Charity as possible to become familiar with the personal writings of their Foundress.

What a wonderful undertaking it was to produce this new edition of the correspondence, the meditations, and the advices of all kinds which she has left us. Indeed, we are discovering, more and more, not only how inseparable she is from Saint Vincent, from whom she received so much, but also the great importance of her own contributions. After a somewhat difficult and uncertain beginning, their collaboration became one of the most marvelous and fruitful witnesses to complementarity between a man and a woman, between a male and a female saint who placed all the resources of their widely divergent personalities at the service of the same ideal.

Nothing is more instructive in this regard than the two conferences of July 3 and July 24, 1660 on the virtues of Louise de Marillac. How moving it is to see Monsieur Vincent, just a few weeks before his own death, thank Our Lord for having preserved him until that moment and express his wonder as the sisters relate their recollections of their Foundress. It is interesting to see him stress certain qualities which he judged characteristic of the person of Mademoiselle Le Gras and particularly important in the vocation of the Daughters of Charity: supernatural prudence, the spirit and practice of poverty, the interior life, humility, gentleness, and above all, love of God and of the Poor.

"Father," said one sister, "I can say nothing else than that the life of Mademoiselle Le Gras is a mirror in which we have only to gaze."

This sentence sums up everything and invites us to find even greater joy in the appearance of this new edition of the writings of Saint Louise during this 350th anniversary year of the birth of the Company. The preceding edition, which we generally referred to as the "Gray Book," came out in 1960 to mark the 300th anniversary of the death of our Founders. It rendered great service as my predecessor, Father Slattery, hoped it would. In the letter that he wrote as a Preface for that edition, he said, "You can but rejoice at seeing the attractive personality of your Holy Mother emerge from the shadows in which her humility had hidden her. But above all, you want those who will know her better in the future, and who esteem her so highly, to find her in those who have the honor of being her Daughters. It is in her writings as well as in those of Saint Vincent that you will find the most perfect expression of your spirit."

For my part, therefore, I wish, with all my heart, that this new edition, in which they have tried to record with greater fidelity the exact words of Saint Louise, be for all the Daughters of Charity a guide for an evermore efficacious service of Our Lord Jesus Christ and of our Lords and Masters, the Poor. By reading it and by meditating on it often, especially during your retreats, you will understand in a very practical way what Monsieur Vincent said of Louise de Marillac in the Conferences mentioned above: "You did not make yourselves, Sisters; it was she who made you and gave birth to you in Our Lord" (*Leonard,* 1273).

Richard McCullen, C.M.
Superior General

TRANSLATOR'S NOTE

In order to fulfill, without delay, the wish expressed by Father McCullen in his Preface that "as many Daughters of Charity as possible become familiar with the personal writings of their Foundress," it was judged well to translate and print at this time that portion of the 1983 French Edition of the *Spiritual Writings of Saint Louise de Marillac* for which there has been no previous English translation, while leaving to a later date any necessary revisions in the correspondence which make up the first part of the new French Edition. The 1972 translation of the *Letters of Saint Louise de Marillac* by Sister Helen Marie Law, D.C. is available to all the English language provinces. It is thus the second part of the new French Edition, entitled "Thoughts", that is presented here.

Since this work is intended primarily as a book of meditation, the references have been simplified and grouped at the end. The interpolations are not indicated in the body of the text and are only mentioned in the notes when the changes or additions are significant. Parentheses indicate titles or dates added by the French editors.

Because of the number of page references found in community writings, such as the *Constitution and Statutes* or the *Echo,* which are taken from the 1983 French Edition, we have added a table indicating the corresponding pages in this English language edition. This should enable the reader to locate the reference easily.

SLS

INTRODUCTION
(FRENCH EDITION)

At the end of the nineteenth century the numerous autographs of Louise de Marillac were classified and carefully regrouped in large, bound collections by Sister Goeffre.

Collection Number One regroups 256 letters from St. Vincent to St. Louise, letters that Monsieur Coste has published in his immense work of fourteen volumes. This collection also contains five other documents: the account of the journey to Nantes, the regulations for Le Mans, and a letter to Brother Ducourneau.

Collection Number Two contains 187 letters written by Louise de Marillac to Monsieur Vincent, and thirty-four letters sent to various people: Priests of the Mission, Ladies of Charity, etc.

Collection Number Three includes the manuscripts of the 329 letters destined for the Daughters of Charity. A certain number of these letters were written by the secretaries (especially Elisabeth Hellot and Mathurine Guérin), but they are signed by St. Louise herself.

Collection Number Four groups the ninety-nine letters that were preciously preserved by the Abbé de Vaux, Vicar General of Angers.

Collection Number Five assembles the other writings of Louise de Marillac: retreats, meditations, diverse thoughts, regulations, conferences . . .

Two other collections, called the Notebooks of Marguerite Chétif, present copies made either by herself or one of the first sisters of autographs handwritten by the Foundress. Marguerite Chétif, named Superioress General by Monsieur Vincent in August, 1660, had asked Mathurine Guerin, Louise de Marillac's secretary for seven years, to send her a collection of Louise's principal virtues in order to follow the Foundress's example in conducting herself.

Mathurine Guérin responds simply: "When I had the happiness of writing her letters, I did not consider them beautiful teachings at the time. However, now I admire the diversity she gave to them. In some, she instills the observance of the Rule, in others fear; in all of them the pure love of God.

"One of the greatest benefits of our Company is the most exact collection that she made and had made of the instructions of our late Most Honored Father. You could say that I am not teaching you anything new since you are just as aware of it as the others; but perhaps they all do not know the charity with which she urged the sisters in their charitable work so that they would not fail . . .

"She often said that a day would come when our dear sisters would be comforted in having the writings of persons that we had had the good fortune of knowing.

"It would take quite a long time if I wanted to specify each of her charitable traits as manifested by the letters which she herself wrote or had written to each sister in particular and to the sisters in general, had

vi

they been kept together. What I could tell you would truly be another instruction for you, my dear Sister. As for me, I have several of them that I keep as relics of her spirit. Nevertheless, if I were commanded to reveal them, I would deny myself these benefits . . ."

In order to preserve the spirit of Louise de Marillac, Marguerite Chétif not only read and meditated upon the letters, but she recopied them in order to transmit the message to all the Daughters of Charity, for whom she was assuming the responsibility.

The copies contain no names of sisters or of cities. The anonymity had to be preserved because several of the Daughters of Charity to whom these letters had been addressed were still living. Thanks to research work undertaken in the last few years at the Archives of the Motherhouse, it was possible to identify several copies with the autographs of Collection Number Three. The letters have been recopied according to their origin from this sister or that house. A series of letters comes from the house at Angers, another from Barbe Angiboust, Anne Hardimont, Laurence Dubois, etc. Several copies could not be identified.

For this new publication, a trial method of chronological classification has been undertaken. The documents without dates are numerous, but by comparing them with the dated letters found in the work of *Coste,* along with the letters received by Louise de Marillac from the Daughters of Charity, the Vincentians and the Administrators, it was possible to date precisely a great number of them. The appearance of the autograph (writing, type of paper) also permits a certain approximation of the period in which the document was written.

When Sister Goeffre classified the different autographs, she assigned to each one a classification number. This number has been faithfully preserved. The letter "L" preceding the number indicates articles of correspondence; the letter "A" indicates diverse thoughts and regulations; the letter "S" indicates documents classified later. The letter "M" designates the copies made by Marguerite Chétif.

This edition presents numerous differences from prior publications because it seemed opportune to return to the complete text of the letters and different writings of Louise de Marillac without regrouping them by themes and without modifying the Seventeenth Century French.

"What a beautiful picture, O my God, this humility, faith, prudence, sound judgment, and constant concern to conform all her actions to those of Our Lord! O Sisters, it is for you to conform your actions to hers and to imitate her in all things."

(Conference on the Virtues of Louise de Marillac, July 24, 1660)

Amiens
BULLES
NEUFVILLE
GOURNAY
BEAUVAIS
CLERMONT
LA BRUYÈRE
RANTIGNY
LIANCOURT
CAUFFRY
PONT-SAINT-MAXENCE
VERNEUIL
CHARS
VILLERS-SOUS-LEU
CHANTILLY
SENLIS
ENNERY
PONTOISE
ASNIÈRES-SUR-OISE
BARON
NANTEUIL
LE HAUDOUIN
CONFLANS HERBLAY
FRANCONVILLE
SANNOIS
MORAINVILLIERS
POISSY
ARGENTEUIL
DAMMARTIN
SAINT-DENIS
COLOMBE
ST-GERMAIN-EN-LAYE
AUBERVILLIERS
LES ALLUETS
NANTERRE
LA CHAPELLE
MAULE
SURESNES
PARIS
ST-CLOUD
GENTILLY
BICETRE
VERSAILLES
ISSY
CLAMART
SUCY-EN-BRIE
FONTENAY-AUX-ROSES
CHAMPLAN
OLLAINVILLE

CONTENTS

Period Prior to The Foundation of The Company of The Daughters of Charity

Period Prior to
The Foundation of
The Company of
The Daughters of Charity

A.2 Light

In the year 1623, on the Feast of Saint Monica, God gave me the grace to make a vow of widowhood should He call my husband to Himself.

On the following Feast of the Ascension, I was very disturbed because of the doubt I had as to whether I should leave my husband, as I greatly wanted to do, in order to make good my first vow[1] and to have greater liberty to serve God and my neighbor.

I also doubted my capacity to break the attachment I had for my director[2] which might prevent me from accepting another, during his long absence, as I feared I might be obliged to do.

I also suffered greatly because of the doubt I experienced concerning the immortality of the soul. All these things caused me incredible anguish which lasted from Ascension until Pentecost.

On the Feast of Pentecost[3], during Holy Mass or while I was praying in the church[4], my mind was instantly freed of all doubt.

I was advised that I should remain with my husband and that a time would come when I would be in a position to make vows of poverty, chastity, and obedience and that I would be in a small community where others would do the same. I then understood that I would be in a place where I could help my neighbor but I did not understand how this would be possible since there was to be much coming and going.

I was also assured that I should remain at peace concerning my director; that God would give me one[5] whom He seemed to show me. It was repugnant to me to accept him; nevertheless, I acquiesced. It seemed to me that I did not yet have to make this change.

My third doubt was removed by the inner assurance I felt that it was God who was teaching me these things and that, believing there is a God, I should not doubt the rest.

I have always believed that I received this grace from the Blessed Bishop of Geneva[6] because, before his death, I had greatly desired to communicate these trials to him and because since that time, I have had great devotion to him and have received many graces through him. On that occasion, I had a reason for believing this to be so, although I cannot now remember it.

A.1 Rule of Life in the World

In the name of God and with His divine assistance, may I live thus!

May the desire for holy poverty always live in my heart in such a manner that, freed from all bonds, I may follow Jesus Christ and serve my neighbor with great humility and gentleness, living under obedience and in chastity all my life and honoring the poverty that Jesus Christ practiced so perfectly.

Upon awakening, may my first thought be of God. May I make acts of adoration, thanksgiving, and abandonment of my will to His most holy will. Reflecting on my lowliness and powerlessness, I shall invoke the grace of the Holy Spirit in which I shall have great confidence for the accomplishment of His will in me, which shall be the sole desire of my heart.

As far as I am able, from Easter to the Feast of All Saints, I shall rise at five-thirty; from the Feast of All Saints until Easter, I shall rise at six o'clock.

Immediately after rising, I shall meditate for an hour or at least three quarters of an hour on a subject taken either from the Gospels or the Epistles to which I shall add a reading from the life of the saint of the day so as to be instructed by a practical example.

After meditation, I shall recite attentively Prime and Terce in honor of Our Lady while preserving the inspirations I received during prayer. Then, if there is any order to be given to the household, I shall take care of it while dressing.

At eight-thirty in the summer and at nine o'clock in the winter, I shall go to Holy Mass. Sometimes my sole intention will be to pray for and with the Church. At other times I will make use of the points for reflection to be found in *Philoteé* or in another book entitled *Dositheé*.

After Mass, I shall finish the recitation of the Office of the Blessed Virgin while continuing to ponder the great love which God showed to us by instituting this Holy Sacrifice.

Upon my return home, at nine-thirty in the summer and at ten o'clock in the winter, I shall work until eleven o'clock. Then, after reading a chapter from a pious book, I shall dine.

Exactly at midday, I shall meditate for a quarter of an hour in order to honor the instant when the Incarnation of the Word took place in the womb of the Virgin Mary.

I shall try never to be idle. Therefore, after these few minutes of meditation, I shall work cheerfully, until four o'clock, either for the Church or for the poor or for my household. If I am obliged to pay a few visits or to receive them, I shall attend to such duties at this time.

At four o'clock, even when I am in the city, provided I am not too involved in some charitable work or some essential social obligation, I shall go to the nearest church to recite Vespers of the Blessed Virgin. During that time, I shall recollect myself so as to be able then to meditate for half an hour. I shall then return home and remain there as far as possible. If there is time, I shall work from after meditation until six o'clock.

I shall have supper at six-thirty. Before this meal, I shall spend from fifteen minutes to half an hour reading. Then, I shall reflect upon what I have read or share my thoughts with my table companions.

After supper, I shall recreate for half an hour and then work for another half hour.

At eight o'clock, I shall retire to make my examination of conscience, humbling myself profoundly for the graces which I may have received from God during the day as well as for the faults which I may have committed, trusting always in His goodness and mercy which are my only hope. Afterward, I shall recite Matins of the Blessed Virgin for the following days. Sometimes, I shall examine my conscience on the manner in which, as a woman desirous of becoming devout, I fulfill the commandments of God and my obligations as a Christian and a Catholic.

Every day I shall recite five decades of the rosary while meditating on one of the mysteries.

I shall strive to remember the presence of God at least four times each hour, exciting within me the desire for His love by means of frequent ejaculatory prayers.

Once a week, I shall read the points which I wrote down about five years ago, so as to remind myself of the obligation I contracted to serve God all my life.

Every first Saturday of the month, I shall renew my vows and my good resolutions by reading my act of consecration either before or after Holy Communion. I have selected Saturday as proof that, because of my weakness and inconstancy, I have chosen the Blessed Virgin as my protectress. Moreover, through her intercession, I hope to honor in her, for the remainder of my life, the preference which God has shown for virginity over the married life.

Therefore, I shall cultivate a special devotion to the Blessed Virgin, my guardian angel, and the Apostles, with the desire of imitating their lives to the best of my ability since they are imitators of our Lord.

I shall recite the hymn "Jesus nostra Redemptor" all year long on the same day of the week as that on which Christmas falls. On the date on which Pentecost falls, I shall say the sequence, "Veni Sancte Spiritus."

I shall receive Holy Communion on Sunday and Tuesday except when special feasts oblige me to choose other days. I shall be faithful to this so as to keep before my mind the realization that I can only desire to serve God if his love draws me.

I shall strive to the best of my ability to overcome my passions, especially vanity and precipitousness. To this end and in honor of the sufferings of Jesus Christ, I shall take the discipline in a spirit of penance two or three times while reciting a Pater in honor of Jesus Chirst, an Ave in praise of the Blessed Virgin and a De Profundis for the souls in Purgatory. I shall wear a hair shirt on the mornings on which I receive Holy Communion and all day Friday.

I shall fast on all Fridays of the year; during Advent and Lent; on the vigils of the feasts of our Lord, the Blessed Virgin and the Apostles, and on all days of fast prescribed by the Church. On days on which there is no fast, I shall take only two meals unless necessity or condescension obliges me to do otherwise.

I would like to spend eight to ten days in retreat twice a year. One would be during the period between the Feast of the Ascension and Pentecost in order to honor the grace which God bestowed on His Church by giving it His Holy Spirit to guide it and by commissioning His Apostles to preach the Gospel to all nations. At this time, I would strive to be particularly attentive to the Word of God and to His law expressed in His commandments. The other days of retreat would be during Advent.

I adore You, O my God, and recognize that You are the author of my existence. Because of the love I owe You, I abandon myself entirely to Your holy will in my life. Although I am filled with powerlessness and reasons for humiliation on account of my sins, I trust in Your mercy. I beg You, because of the love You have for Your creatures, to send the assistance of the Holy Spirit so as to produce the full effect of the plan which Your holy will has had, from all eternity, for my soul and for all souls redeemed by the blood of Jesus Christ.

A.13 An Interior Trial

(c. 1621)

On the Feast of Saint Thomas, I fell into a state of depression which lasted all day. The sight of my own abjection led me to consider myself as a mass of pride and self-love. I experienced discouragement, annihilation of myself, and desertion by God which I had merited because of my infidelities. My heart was so depressed that the force of my emotions sometimes resulted in physical pain. When I considered the esteem which, at times, others mistakenly accord me, I felt that I was unworthy to have the holy will of God accomplished in me.

On the following Tuesday, still experiencing the same trial, I looked upon myself as the object of divine justice. Holy Communion and all the other graces which God had bestowed upon me were to be the means of revealing His goodness in carrying out His justice. Once I had accepted this reality, I felt somewhat at peace. I took as the subject of my meditation: the peace of God which surpasses all understanding.

A.15b   On the Desire to Give Herself to God
(c.1622)

On the Feast of Saint Sebastian, Martyr, I felt a strong desire to give myself to God to fulfill His holy will for the remainder of my life. I offered to Him the inspiration which He had given me to seal this desire by vow once I had obtained permission. For the rest of the day, I meditated on the mercy of God to His creatures as seen in all the good accomplished by His saints. Their deeds appeared even greater to me when I reflected upon my personal experience of the weakness of human nature.

The following Saturday, I begged God earnestly to make known what His goodness desired of me. On Sunday, the awareness of my infidelities to God so filled me with confusion that I was prepared not to receive Holy Communion without first going to confession. I was particularly ashamed of the fact that, on a day on which I was to receive Holy Communion, I had failed so miserably in recollection and had resisted the inspiration to mortify myself two or three times. I had stifled the very idea of mortification by blocking it completely from my mind. The only thing that prevented me from abstaining from Holy Communion was the reminder that I had been forbidden to do so. All day, I suffered from great interior trials.

On the following Tuesday, the Feast of the Conversion of Saint Paul, I reflected on how Jesus destroyed all the obstacles to the operation of His divine will both in Saint Paul and in the entire Gentile community. This thought produced such a sudden painful sensation within me that I was almost unable to make my confession. The pain was so great that, if I had said and done what I felt impelled to do, I believe that . . .

I was ordered to receive Holy Communion every Saturday to thank Jesus Christ for His assistance and that of His Holy Mother.

On the last Sunday of January, I meditated on the greatness of God. I reflected on Jesus, in the Crib. The truth of His Being was alone sufficient for His Eternal Glory yet, in conformity to the will of His Father for our Redemption, He despised the riches and grandeur of this world so as to detach us from the things of earth.

As I meditated on the Gospel of the Sower, I realized that there was no good soil in me. Therefore I desired to sow, in the heart of Jesus, all the actions of my heart and soul in order that they may grow by sharing in His merits. Henceforth, I shall exist only through Him and in Him since He has willed to lower Himself to assume human nature.

A.31 On Fidelity in the Service of Jesus

As I contemplated Christ who had brought eternal joy to the world and saw Him filled with sorrow, I realized that His sadness did not come from within but was caused by His love for me. Not only did He grieve at the thought of all the sufferings He was to endure but His love was wounded by the foreknowledge of my ingratitude and infidelities. This meditation should lead me to greater devotion in His service and enable me to honor His holy sadness by the little services I render to Him and especially by greater fidelity to my rule of life, since He is offended by disorder.

If I do not want to slumber in sloth for the rest of my life, I must lovingly express this desire to Jesus with the confidence that He will draw me out of it when I am disposed to let Him act in me. This will happen when, having no life of my own, I recognize my own powerlessness and become entirely dependent upon God who is surely calling me to a closer union with Him by abandoning anything that separates me from Him.

A.3 Act of Consecration

I, the undersigned, in the presence of the eternal God, having considered that, on the day of my holy Baptism, I was vowed and dedicated to my God to be His daughter and that, notwithstanding, I have repeatedly offended Him by acting contrary to His holy will; having considered, also, the great mercy, love, and gentleness with which this kind God has always preserved in me the desire to serve Jesus Christ despite my almost continual culpable resistance to His graces which, throughout my negligent and ungrateful life, He has lavished upon me, unworthy and frail creature that I am ...

Finally, entering into myself, I detest with all my heart the iniquities of my past life which render me guilty of high treason against the Divine Majesty and of the death of Jesus Christ; because of this, I am more deserving of damnation than Lucifer. However, trusting in the infinite mercy of my God, I implore, with all my heart, pardon and entire absolution both for the sins which I have confessed and for those that I cannot recall. I ask pardon particularly for the contempt I have shown for His goodness by abusing the sacraments. I sincerely repent of all these sins, once again, relying on the merit of the death of the Savior of my soul as on the only foundation of my hope. In virtue of this, I affirm and renew the sacred profession made to God for me at my Baptism. I irrevocably resolve to love and serve Him with greater fidelity and to give myself entirely to Him. To this end, I also

11

renew my vow of widowhood and my resolution to practice the most holy virtues of humility, obedience, poverty, suffering, and charity in order to honor these same virtues in Jesus Christ who, in His love, has often called me to imitate Him.

Promising never again to offend God by any part of my being and to abandon myself entirely to the designs of Divine Providence and to the accomplishment of His will in me, I sacrifice and dedicate myself to God and to the fulfillment of His holy will which I choose as my supreme consolation.

If, on account of my usual weakness, I should fail to keep these holy resolutions, which I beg God, in His goodness, not to permit, I implore the Holy Spirit, from this very moment, to grant me the grace of immediate conversion because I never wish to remain for an instant in a state which is displeasing to God. This is my irrevocable intention which I confirm in the presence of my God, of the Blessed Virgin, of my guardian angel, and of all the saints, here before the Church Militant which accepts this consecration in the person of my spiritual director. Since this spiritual father takes the place of God for me on earth, I entreat him, by his charitable guidance, to help me to be faithful to my resolutions and to the accomplishment of the holy will of God by my obedience to him in this matter.

O my God, deign to confirm my consecration and my holy resolutions and to accept them as a fragrant offering! Since You inspired me to present these gifts to You, grant me the grace of perfecting them. You are my God and my All. I recognize You as such and adore You, the one true God in three Persons, now and forever.

May Your Love and that of Jesus Crucified be eternally exalted!

Louise de Marillac

A.4   Oblation to the Blessed Virgin

(c. 1626)

Most Holy Virgin, deign to take my son and me into Your care. Welcome the choice I make of You as our protectress. Accept my vows and my prayers as well as my heart which I give entirely to you so as to glorify God for the choice He made of you to be the Mother of His Son. Because of this divine action, your conception was immaculate since the Father applied to you the anticipated merit of the death of Jesus Christ. May all generations to come bless your birth. May your holy and pure life, devoted to the service of the temple, be as an example to virgins who have the happiness of imitating your untarnished vow of virginity. May persons united by the will of God in holy matrimony honor your pure marriage by their submission to, their dependence upon, and their confidence in the Providence of God. May they imitate the limitless virtues which you practiced during the years of the hidden life of your Son, Jesus Christ, especially your great humility which made you ever open to the action of God in you and to your place in the divine plan. May widows learn from you what God is asking of them so that they may honor by practice and example the sweet tranquillity of your soul as you stood at the foot of the Cross, and your detachment from all earthly things during the period following the Ascension. May they, likewise, imitate your pure love of God and your zeal for the salvation of souls to which you devoted the remainder of your life in perfect fidelity to the spirit of Jesus, my Savior.

Although I am but an unworthy sinner, I beg you, Holy Virgin, to allow me to unite myself to your merits so that I may glorify God for the glory He will receive from you by the pleasure He takes in your holy soul and by the revelation of the plenitude of His divinity which operated so extraordinarily in you. Blessed was your dear heart, filled with love, which, after great interior suffering, gave death to your holy body, separating it from your soul so full of merit. May your beautiful soul be forever triumphant, elect among millions, because of your faithful accomplish-ment of the designs of God. May your blessed body, once again united to your soul, be in everlasting glory because of the testimonies of love it will receive from the most Holy Trinity for all eternity.

I am entirely yours, most Holy Virgin, that I may more perfectly belong to God. Teach me, therefore, to imitate your holy life by fulfilling the designs of God in my life. I very humbly beg you to assist me. You know my weakness. You see the desires of my heart. Supply for my powerlessness and negligence by your prayers. Since your dear Son, my Redeemer, is the source of the heroic virtue of which you gave the example during your life on earth, unite the spirit of my actions to His for the glory of His holy love. May all creatures pay homage to your greatness and look upon you as the sure means for reaching God. May they love you above all other pure creatures and render you the glory you deserve as the beloved Daughter of the Father, Mother of the Son, and wor-thy Spouse of the Holy Spirit.

Most Holy Virgin, have pity on all souls redeemed by the Son of God, your Son, Jesus Christ. Offer to the Divine Justice your pure body which furnished the blood which He shed for our Redemption so that His merits may be applied to the souls of the dying and effect in them complete conversion. Procure for us, through your intercession, all that we need to give glory to God in the fullness of heavenly beatitude and to enjoy the blessedness which your dear presence imparts to the saints who are now with you in glory.

A.38   On the End of the Congregation of the
Mission   (Before 1628)

That the principal end of the Association[7] be knowledge of oneself and contempt for the things of the world, practiced by the resolution to serve the Parishes, in submission and obedience to the Pastors, while renouncing all benefices and honors.

In the design of serving the Church, it shall have a knowledge of God, recognizing Him as sovereignly worthy of being fittingly honored. To this end, each one in particular shall give himself entirely to work for the salvation of souls insofar as he can hope to do so by the love of God. This work will be greatly advanced by their example and their instructions on the duties of a Christian as well as by the grace of the sacraments worthily administered in the Church. This will happen and the glory of God will be greater when the only priests are good priests.

Moreover, they shall honor the Blessed Trinity by great union among themselves. This union shall be neither constrained nor forced but always maintained by gentle necessity which cordiality transforms into mutual affection. By a communication of the Holy Spirit, they shall enter into a holy relationship with the Son of God who, by personally detaching Himself, as it were, from His Father, willed to take our flesh for the salvation of the human race. Likewise, they shall be completely detached from anything that could prevent them from working toward this same end, for the glory of God.

A.39 Motives to Pray for the Congregation of the Mission (Before 1628)

To present the end of the Association to the Blessed Virgin, pointing out that it renders the greatest possible glory to God in the person of His Son since it seeks, firstly, to work for the perfection of priests who take His place on earth and who have the honor and the power to render Him present so frequently in the Sacrament of the Altar and, secondly, to reanimate the hierarchy of the Church with its primitive fervor.

To implore Mary to offer to God the way by which He is calling them, that is: by honoring the Cross and by imitating the Son of God who, in the abjection of His Passion, united the human race to God.

Since their end is also to work for the salvation of souls and to keep themselves always in lowly positions and submissive to others, to ask Mary, by her intercession, to obtain the perfection of this spirit for them and for their successors.

To beg the Blessed Virgin to obtain for them from God the grace to eliminate any human considerations in their establishment and, should there have been any in the past, to destroy them by her prayers so that God may be pleased to guide them by His Holy Spirit and to look upon their Association as truly His work.

A.17 Fears and Consolations Experienced Concerning Holy Communion

From time to time, especially on solemn feast days, the sight of my abjection, occasioned by my faults and my infidelities to God, causes me to fear to receive Holy Communion. Sometimes, I experience an unwillingness to see such a good God come into such a miserable place. At other times, I am afraid that my audacity in approaching this most Holy Sacrament will draw down some exemplary punishment upon me from the Divine Justice. On the Feast of All Saints, I was particularly overwhelmed by the thought of my lowliness, when my soul was made to understand that my God wanted to come to me. However, He did not wish to come into some temporary dwelling but to a place that was rightly His and which belonged entirely to Him. Therefore, I could not refuse Him entrance. As a living soil, I had to welcome Him joyfully as the true possessor of my soul and simply acquiesce to Him, giving Him my heart as the throne of His Majesty. With the disciples, I desire to hear the precepts of the Holy Gospel of the day.

A.7   Retreat Meditations

(c. 1628)[8]

First Day

Since God had no other plan in view when He created our souls, which so far surpass all other creatures, than to possess them entirely, I intend, with the help of His grace, to give myself willingly and completely to Him and to avoid all those occasions that might prevent me from doing so.

I must greatly esteem the means which I have for reaching the end for which my soul was created. Time is one such means but God has others, as yet unknown to me. I desire always to abandon myself to Him so as to allow Him to employ them. I should also have great respect for the reality that, once I have attained this end, my soul will have the honor of rendering eternal gratitude, glory, and love to God.

The knowledge of the love that God has for us in creating our souls so that they could be entirely possessed by Him, rejoice in Him, and glorify Him, is a greater motive for loving Him than all the benefits of creation. However, we must also venerate this grace in others. That is why I must honor and love them and strive to help them to attain their eternal salvation so that they may reach the goal for which they were created.

Second Day

Although subjection to sin is very damaging, it is, nevertheless, a sign of the excellence of the soul and will never prove detrimental so long as God does not withhold the grace necessary to preserve us from it. Therefore, with the help of His grace, I shall have great confidence in His goodness and keep before me the image of my weakness so that I will fear, not so much the punishment due to sin, which is a sign of the Divine Sovereignty, as the fact that sin separates us from God and from His love.

The greatest proof of the enormity of sin is the fact that it has brought death even to our bodies. Jesus Christ Himself was subject to it in order to satisfy for our sins. This leads me to believe that God has great esteem for pain and suffering since, by means of them, Jesus Christ expiated the sin of our first parents. Our Savior is gentle and merciful to us until the last hour when the soul enters Eternity. Then he exercises His justice toward those who have died. They remain in the state in which they were at the moment of their death. This gives me reason to fear but it also gives me the desire, without flattering myself, to carry out what God is asking of me. I shall seek help to try to discern this.

I shall willingly accept death and the reason behind this physical annihilation since, in a certain sense, the pain it entails satisfies for sin. I must have a great horror for sin although I do not feel its presence in my soul where it actually is. Because of this lack of knowledge, I shall have great confidence in God that He will deliver me from those sins into which I ordinarily fall with no thought of the offense I am committing against God.

Third Day

The soul that has loved God rejoices to see itself at the particular judgment when the hour of death has come, but it is a sorrowful occasion for one who has not loved Him. Since in the Providence of God I have not been able to make any particular resolution, I shall place my trust in His mercy, abandoning myself entirely to His goodness, knowing that He will save me without such resolutions.

My ignorance and my powerlessness to desire or to resolve to practice particular virtues causes me to attach myself strongly and perseveringly to Jesus Christ Crucified, so that the joy which I now feel in meditating on the Last Judgment, where I see my Savior reigning alone and acknowledged by all, may not, on that day, turn to shame because of my sins and ingratitude which have merited hell although I was not conscious of this.

May the glory of the true humanity of Jesus Christ appear since it is as Man, although united to the Divinity, that He will judge us at both the particular and the general judgment. Moreover, He is a judge Who can neither be corrupted nor deceived. Love alone can win Him. I must ask this of Him and recall my fear of the sins which are now hidden from me but will then be exposed for my shame if I do not now humble myself and repent.

Fourth Day

The pains of hell are caused by eternal banishment from the presence of God. In order to avoid them, after confiding myself to the divine mercy, I shall try to have, instead of the continual hatred of God, the forgetfulness of grace, and the rage against others of the damned, a deep love for God in this life which will be shown by practicing His goodness, gentleness, and charity toward my neighbor.

As soon as human nature had sinned, the Creator, who wanted to repair this fault by a great act of pure love, ordered, in the Council of His Divinity, that one of the three Persons should become Man. By so doing, He gave proof of deep, true humility. This caused me to be ashamed of my pride. Part of my vanity is surely due to ignorance since, properly speaking, humility is the knowledge of truth. This is why it is possible to recognize it in God. But, my soul, what is God asking of us by the Incarnation of His dear Son other than gratitude for our Redemption? Just as He personally left heaven to be united to the earth, so He wants us to willingly abandon the earth of our sensuality so as to be united to the essence of His Divinity.

God never showed greater love for His creatures than when He resolved to become Man since all the graces that He subsequently bestowed on us depend on this initial act. This teaches me that we must have a great and special love for our enemies and do all in our power to procure their salvation.

Fifth Day

The Son of God was not satisfied with promising to redeem us or with becoming Man. But He willed to come into this world in a manner not at all consistent

20

with His grandeur. He came as humbly as can be imagined so that we might be more free to approach Him. We must do this with a respect commensurate with His humility. This humble act shows us how great this virtue is in God since all the actions He performs outside of the Godhead are greatly beneath Him.

Our Lord showed even greater evidence of His love in the conversion of sinners than in the continuation of His graces to the just. This is seen in the case of the Samaritan Woman where everything He said and did was a manifestation of love. This should lead me to place great confidence and trust in His goodness, knowing that He will grant me His holy love at the end. However, I must work for this and listen to His Word.

Sixth Day

The infinite perfection of God contains within itself the perfection of all His creatures who, by necessity or willingly, act only through His power. I should humble myself, therefore, because in a certain sense, His permissive will causes Him to contribute to my iniquities. Consequently, in order to be no longer the occasion of such an evil, I shall, with the help of His grace, keep myself in His presence, which I hope never to leave, although I am not always consciously aware of it.

The infinite goodness and wisdom of God leave the soul free to draw on the infinite sources of His love. He is so good that He communicates His prodigious love to all. This should keep my soul very humble and dependent on the divine goodness.

I must be mindful not to seek tenderness or spiritual consolation as a motive for serving God. Rather, I accept all the dryness and lack of consolation for which my soul is destined. I offer myself in total abandonment to God to endure all the temptations it will please Him to send, and to live and to die in this state if such be His holy will.

Seventh Day

I must practice interior humility by a desire for abjection and exterior humility by willingly accepting all the occasions which occur for humbling myself. I shall do this in order to honor the true and real humility of God Himself in whom I shall find the strength to overcome my pride, to combat my frequent outbursts of impatience, and to acquire charity and gentleness toward my neightbor. Thus I shall honor the teaching of Jesus Christ who told us to learn of Him to be gentle and humble of heart.

I shall make the Way of the Cross as a penance and shall receive Holy Communion tomorrow.

A.21 Thoughts on the Passion of Our Lord

Honor the condition of Our Lord Jesus Christ after His Resurrection: purgatory of desire after God the Father had received His spirit; purgatory of human nature in Him.

Fidelity to Jesus Christ on the Cross, who willed to fulfill the Scriptures. When Jesus knew that He had endured all the pain which the Scriptures had foretold. He increased His own sufferings saying, "I thirst."

The demands of the Bad Thief show me that we do not know how to fully appreciate the value of suffering, while the conduct of the Good Thief teaches me the merit to be found in honoring justice, confessing the truth, and praying.

I gave myself to God to accept the designs of His Providence if He willed me to continue, for the remainder of Lent, in a state of interior abandonment

22

and even affliction so as to honor the sufferings of Jesus Christ which the Church places before our eyes.

Jesus thirsted on the Cross after He saw that all had been accomplished. His afflicted body, like a deer, sought the relief of water. He suffered a double thirst: that of His body and that of His spirit. He bears witness to this by crying out simply, "I thirst." His refusal to swallow the drink offered to Him reveals His desire to reunite His divine Person to the Father and the Holy Spirit. His third cry expresses His thirst to apply His merits to all souls created for paradise.

He willed to forgo even necessities so as to use every moment of His life to the fullest. Listen to Him, O my soul, as if He were speaking to you alone, "I thirst for your faithful love."

Death has lost its sting because it has not separated the divinity from the blessed body of Jesus Christ nor deprived it of grace.

The jeering of the crowds reveals those who do not believe in Jesus Christ and who refuse to do good without miracles. By forgiving them, Jesus shows that there is no place in Him for contempt or revenge. In asking pardon for His enemies, He excuses them.

The admirable work which took place at the moment of the Redemption of the human race is manifested in the words of our Lord, "My God, my God, why have you forsaken me?" This cry shows us that His divine Person suffered, at that moment, from an extraordinary sense of separation which led Him to address His Father as "My God." By the infinite merit of this instant, the human race is in full possession of the power to be reunited with its God if it will but make use of the means to do so. "My God, my God, why have you forsaken me?" Jesus no longer says "My Father." Thus He reveals the suffering of the

Son of God and the sense of abandonment of the Second Person of the Blessed Trinity. The Father forsakes His Son so as to welcome back the human race.

"I thirst." Jesus addresses these words to us so that we might understand that His death is not sufficient to save us if we do not apply the merits to ourselves and this can only be done by the personal consent of each individual soul . . . He does not address His Father. He does not ask for something to drink. He simply cries out, "I thirst." . . .

A.9 Retreat

I must depend completely upon God and show no greater resistance to Him now than I did when He created me.

I must use my entire being to know God in His works and to recognize Him by love.

I desired to no longer subsist of myself. After having been continuously sustained by the grace of God, it seemed to me that all that I am is but grace. I implored God to draw these graces to Himself and thus I would be totally His.

To love abjection since God is to be found there. Jesus teaches us this by His birth. He wanted us to know that this abjection filled heaven with astonishment and gave glory to the Father. However, I must unite my miserable, weak self-abnegation to His glorious abjection.

To give life to Jesus in my heart by love, thus rendering Him present in me. This presence will be the sole object of my attention as it was for the Blessed Virgin at the Crib.

The means to imitate Jesus at the moment of His birth is to have my soul completely united to God and my mind filled with true knowledge of my own nothingness.

To admire, on the one hand, the true humanity of Jesus and, on the other, His divine works and the word of God which He spoke. To thank Him for the grace given to obedient souls to know the truth of His words.

God demands great purity of intention from those who serve Him. Therefore, I must, in no way, seek to derive glory from any action. God must be guiding my intentions for me to have attained the degree of purity necessary to realize that there was a lack of it in my desire for the graces of God.

To imitate the simplicity of Jesus when He told the Jews that they wanted to put Him to death.

To admire the kindness of Jesus in teaching and putting up with the Jews. To listen to the word of God spoken in my heart.

To have recourse to God to eliminate sin from my life since He is willing to assist us.

To avoid anything that would breach charity to my neighbor. To struggle courageously against my evil inclinations.

To take care of the service and glory of God and He will take care of me in all things.

To remove the obstacles to the serenity He desires to see in me.

To wait for God to visit me during this time of rest and to say to me, as to the holy men of old, "Sin no more!"

To seek Jesus in the Tomb, that is to say, in affliction and abandonment. But truly to seek Him without undue concern about the cause of this feeling of separation from Him. To have great confidence so as to overcome any difficulty that might stand in the way of my finding Him. To admire the goodness of the Providence of God.

To have great distrust in myself although the reasons for such distrust are not always apparent. To recall that the weight of my ingratitude for the goodness of God had, at one time, been such a heavy burden for me that His Providence had to come to my aid and permit me, once again, to make good resolutions in His presence, which seemed to me to be a pure abuse of His mercy.

A.10 Resolutions for the Period from Ascension to Pentecost (c. 1630)

To keep my mind as fully occupied as possible in honoring the glory which the holy humanity of our Lord receives in heaven, remembering the way in which He lived on earth, with the desire to imitate Him.

To consider the Blessed Virgin accepting to be deprived of her Son and remaining on earth for the good of Christians, with the desire to remain here myself so long as it is the good pleasure of God for me to accomplish His holy will in this life. I shall also often recall the dispositions of the holy Apostles as they prepared for the coming of the Holy Spirit, especially their serenity in awaiting Him.

To mortify myself interiorly and exteriorly in so far as I am able. To offer to God, several times each day, the charity which He put into the heart of Blessed Francis de Sales and to ask through the intercession of this saint, that the designs of the holy will of God may be fulfilled in me.

The reading of the eighth and ninth books of the *Treatise on the Love of God*[9] with gentleness, calm, and attention.

To request to be warned of my faults, to confess them, and to ask for a penance.

A.50 Visits to the Confraternities of Asnières and Saint-Cloud

(Feb. 1630)[10]

On Ember Wednesday preceding Christmas, I left for Asnières. I was fearful of making this trip because of my ailments, but the thought of the obedience which was sending me on this trip strengthened me considerably. At Holy Communion, on that day, I was moved to make an act of faith, and this sentiment stayed with me for a long time. It seemed to me that God would grant me health so long as I believed that He could sustain me, despite all appearances, and that He would do so if I often reflected on the faith that enabled Saint Peter to walk on the waters.

Throughout my trip, I seemed to be acting without any contribution on my part; and I was greatly consoled by the thought that God wished that, despite my unworthiness, I should help my neighbor to know Him.

I left on the Feast of Saint Agatha, February 5, to go to Saint-Cloud. At the moment of Holy Communion, it seemed to me that our Lord inspired me to receive Him as the Spouse of my soul and that this Communion was a manner of espousal. I felt myself more closely united to Him by this consideration which was extraordinary for me. I also felt moved to leave everything to follow my Spouse; to look upon Him as such in the future; and to bear with the difficulties I might encounter as part of the community of His goods.

God permitting, I wanted to have a Mass celebrated on that day because it was the anniversary of my marriage.[11] I abstained, however, wishing to perform an act of poverty and to depend solely upon God in the action I was about to undertake. I had not expressed my wish to my confessor who celebrated the Mass at which I received Holy Communion.

27

However, as he came out on the altar, the thought came to him to celebrate it for me as an alms and to say the nuptial Mass.

A.51 Visits to the Confraternities of Sannois, Franconville, Herblay, and Conflans

Saturday Noon

For the past year there has been no Procurator for the Confraternity of Sannois. Nevertheless, a good man has continued to keep a written record of revenues and expenditures and he is now willing to accept this position, if elected to it. The Ladies of the Charity have let their zeal cool a bit. Often they do not visit the sick on the days for which they are responsible because the Treasurer is so good-hearted that she cooks the food for those who should be doing it that day. Also, she and the Superioress are sometimes satisfied with giving money to the sick. They also give money to some needy persons and often fail to buy meat. They make the sick do without eggs or something else they would have liked.

These Ladies, or at least the majority of them, go months without receiving Holy Communion. They need to have their zeal reenkindled by a sermon when a priest is sent for the election of the Procurator. The Superioress was willing to have the safe in her home and she had given both keys to the Treasurer.

They are having difficulty in serving the sick. They say that there is no need for a Charity at Sannois to serve only those who have nothing since there are none, or practically none, in this condition. However, they claim that there are many who have little and the little they have is used to meet their own needs so that they would prefer to die of hunger rather than sell what they have and help one another.

Thursday evening

In Franconville, the Procurator of the Charity has lent money to twenty-five persons with no guarantee of repayment. He seemed disposed to continue this practice as the occasion might arise. The officers do not dare oppose him in this because he is very autocratic. The officers were replaced by election a long time ago but continue to fulfill their functions. It is to be feared that, if they continue to do so much longer, it will be impossible to replace them and put others into these positions. They sometimes give money to the sick when their relatives want to care for them and let them go without meat when it is difficult to obtain. Many of the Ladies spend money on their appointed day according to their own whims and pay little attention to the Rule.

Friday morning

In Herblay, the Ladies of Charity are still in their first fervor. Nevertheless, they find it difficult to seek alms and complain that the curate had promised to have the charity to say Holy Mass for them without a stipend. The Treasurer does not keep records. They have resolved to carry a candle in the funeral procession of a deceased member, to receive Holy Communion on the appointed days, and to observe faithfully the other points of the Rule.

Tuesday after Vespers

In Conflans, no Procurator was ever elected for the Charity. Because of illness, the service of the sick stopped a long time ago. A priest records expenses but he does not enter revenues because, he claims, there are not enough to be significant. There is no more linen. The treasury contains about fifty pounds. Upon the advice of the Pastor, money has been given to the sick. The sick often have to go without meat. However, their intentions are good. All have promised to observe the Rule. Some have agreed to provide linen.

A.46 Rule of the Charity
The End for which the Confraternity of Charity is to be Instituted

It shall be instituted in the Parish Church, in the Blessed Sacrament Chapel, which is a symbol of union. Its end is to honor our Lord Jesus Christ, as its Patron, and His Holy Mother; to assist the sick poor of the Parish where it is established: spiritually, by seeing to it that those who die leave this world in a good state and that those who recover resolve never again to offend God, and corporally, by administering the necessary food and remedies to them; finally, to fulfill the ardent desire of our Lord that we love one another.

Patron of the Confraternity

It shall be our Lord Jesus Christ who is Charity.

Persons to be Admitted

It shall be composed of a stated number of virtuous women and girls. Married women shall be admitted only with the consent of their husbands while young girls must have the approval of their father and mother. They shall be called Servants of the Poor.

Officers

The aforementioned Servants of the Poor shall elect three of their number to direct their Confraternity with the approval of the Pastor or of his delegate. One of those elected shall be the Directress or Superioress. The other two shall be first and second Assistant.

The Directress

The Directress shall do all in her power to see to it that the present rule is faithfully observed; that each Servant of the Poor accomplishes her duty; and that the sick poor are well served. She shall procure additional revenue for the Confraternity; receive the sick poor who are to be cared for by the Confraternity after they have been to confession and received Holy Communion; and she shall keep one of the keys to the safe where the funds of the Confraternity are kept.

The Assistants

They shall serve as advisers to the Directress. One shall handle current funds and keep the second key to the safe. The other shall oversee the goods of the Charity and the care of the linen.

Duties of Each Servant of the Poor

They shall look upon the sick poor as their own children, God having made them their mothers; they shall serve them in the manner set forth in this Rule on the days appointed; they shall assist at the Low Mass which the Confraternity shall have celebrated on one of the first days of each month, selecting the day of the week on which the Feast of the Nativity of our Lord falls that year. Their intention shall be to be united in the charity of our Lord. Those who can conveniently do so shall go to confession and receive Holy Communion on these days. They shall all pray for the deceased Servants of the Poor as well as for the poor whom they have assisted. Each morning and evening, they shall say the Pater and the Ave for the preservation of the Confraternity, for its spiritual and temporal growth, and for their benefactors. They shall arrange to have a sermon preached on the first feast of each month both to encourage them to persevere in their good works and to persuade others who will hear it to be generous to the Confraternity.

Manner in which the Servants of the Poor should serve the Sick

Each Servant of the Poor shall serve, on her appointed day, in the manner indicated here. When it is her turn, she shall purchase meat from the butcher, bread from the baker, and wine from the inn. She shall keep a written record of her purchases. She shall prepare the meal and bring it to the sick who should eat at nine o'clock in the morning. She shall do the same for supper which should be served around five o'clock in the evening. After she has finished her service of the day, she shall contact the Lady who will follow her to serve the poor the next day. She shall give her accounts and inform her of the number and condition of the sick.

Manner in which the Sick are to be Fed

Each sick person is to receive four or five ounces of lamb or veal with each meal, as much bread as he can reasonably eat, and half a glass of wine (Paris measure). On fast days, they shall have two eggs with each meal and bouillons made with butter and egg whites.

Mutual Charity among Themselves

They shall cherish one another as Sisters who profess to honor the spirit of our Lord by the practice of charity which is the virtue He practiced most perfectly on earth and which He most strongly recommended to His followers. To this end they shall visit one another and assist one another in sickness and in health. They shall pray for one another especially in case of sickness or death, as has been mentioned. In short, they should do all in their power to help one another to leave this world in a good state. They do all this, however, with no obligation binding by sin, either mortal or venial.

Election of Officers and Financial Reports

The election of officers shall take place every two years on the first work day of the year. They shall be elected by a majority of votes of the Servants of the Poor. There shall be a special election when an officer dies or has been absent for a long time. A financial report shall be given the same day in the presence of the Pastor or his delegate. At the same time, the Treasurer shall turn over any remaining funds to the person elected to replace her. At this time, the second Assistant shall give the goods of the Confraternity to her successor.

A.19 On the Love Which God Has Shown to Us in the Mystery of the Redemption

The Triune God, in the unity of His essence, created me for Himself alone. He has loved me from all eternity. Seeing that I could neither come into being or subsist without Him, since He is my first and only origin, He wants also to be my end and, indeed, He must be. Therefore, he created all things as means to enable me to reach Him just as river banks guide waters to their source. Thus, I must honor and love all creatures because of the design of God in creating them.

The good God saw that, through too many attachments, I had often abused all these means and especially the noblest of them, my will. Thus, He asks me to give my will to Him. I shall do this by entire confidence and abandonment to His most holy will. However, I continue to abuse His means. It is then that the invention of His Divine Love teaches me and permits me to attach myself to the greatest means He has given me for reaching my end, the most holy humanity of His Son. With the help of His grace, this sacred humanity shall be the only example for my life.

I recognize my unworthiness and misery and the fact that it is by His goodness and His love alone, that He wills to be my strength in the painful circumstances which I encounter in His service. I felt great consolation at a glimpse of my poverty but I realize that in this I had neither the horror for sin that I must have nor the necessary dread of the punishment it merits and which the fallen angels and evil men of yore already suffer. Nevertheless, I must rightly fear the judgment of God which will be even more rigorous for me. Like the angels and our first parents, I must obey God because He is God. However, I have received much more than they. I have knowledge of the great love God has for us which was hidden from them. Moreover, the special proofs of His love which His mercy has accorded to me add even greater weight to my sins because of my ingratitude.

The Blessed Virgin is the one who most desired the proof of the love of God revealed in the Redemption I shall implore her to obtain for me sincere gratitude for this great good and the fear necessary to make good use of it.

A.29 On Charity

The person who does not love does not know God, for God is Charity. The cause of love is esteem for the good in the thing loved. Since God is most perfect in the unity of His essence, He is love in the eternity of this essence by the knowledge He has of His own perfection. The love of creatures enters into the nature of this love. But the effects are attached to the will in the practice of charity either toward God or toward the neighbor. This practice of charity is so powerful that it gives us the knowledge of God, not as He is in Himself, but we penetrate so deeply into the mystery of God and His greatness that we may say that the greater our charity the greater our participation in this divine light which will inflame us with the fire of Holy Love for all eternity. Therefore, I want to do everything in my power to practice this Holy Love and to rid my heart of any bitterness which might wound it.

Souls destined by God to a state of suffering should love it greatly and be persuaded that, without His special assistance, they could not be faithful to Him. It seems to me that we have proof of this in the sanctification of Saint John in the womb of his mother. This was an anticipated grace which gave him the strength to respond to the designs of God for his soul. The first sign that God gives that His goodness intends to call a soul to Himself by the path of suffering is similar to this sanctification because it is a rebirth in grace. Since we often receive this grace after the age of reason, its continuation depends entirely upon us. However, I lost it by preferring self-love to the love of God, therefore, I now ask Him for it again with great humility and shame.

God, Who has granted me so many graces, led me to understand that it was His holy will that I go to Him by way of the Cross. His goodness chose to mark me with it from my birth and He has hardly ever left me, at any age, without some occasion of suffering. Since grace had many times enabled me to esteem and desire this state, I trusted that His goodness would, again today, grant me a new grace to carry out His holy will. I begged Him, with all my heart, to place me in this state no matter how painful I found it.

After confession, reflecting on my misery, not so

much on account of the faults I had confessed as on account of those which I had unwillingly failed to acknowledge or had not expressed clearly, I felt as if all my sins had remained on my soul to such an extent that I was overwhelmed by a sort of physical awareness of having sinned. My love and esteem for the Divine Presence caused me to believe that I should not or could only with great pain permit my Lord to enter a place so unworthy of His grandeur. However, since I had been ordered to do so, I received Holy Communion. Immediately after the reception of the Host, my heart was filled with sorrow for having been preoccupied with creatures and having sought their love and consolation. I was grieved by this because my conscience reproached me by reminding me of how often His goodness had moved me to desire Him alone. And, indeed, He had even revealed that such was His will. This led me to renew my resolution to make Him my All and I asked God to put me in a state where this would be possible.

A.6 Retreat

The first day to reflect on the purgative way; the next four, on the life of Jesus Christ; and the last on the coming of the Holy Spirit.

— The goal of creation; obstacles to the attainment of this goal; summary of my meditation.

— Second day, the particular judgment; the Prodigal Son; summary of my meditation.

— Third day, the design which God has had from all eternity for my soul; the obstacles to the accomplishment of this design; summary of my meditation. Then, examination of conscience particularly on the resolution I made during my last retreat and the advice I had received for putting it into practice.

— Fourth day, the Council of the Holy Trinity on the Incarnation; the Nativity; summary of my meditation.

— Fifth day, the Prayer in the Garden of Olives; the Crowning with Thorns; summary of my meditation.

— Sixth day, the Resurrection; the coming of the Holy Spirit; summary of my meditation.

— Then, the two final days, the Divine Attributes; conclude with a meditation on Paradise. Do all in a spirit of gentleness and love.

Outline written by Saint Vincent

— First Meditation, The end for which we have been created and the means for attaining it, which are all created things.

— Second Meditation, A summary of the preceding one.

— Third Meditation, The obstacles that could prevent us from attaining the end for which we were created, which are sin and the great spiritual and corporal evils caused by sin; The first effect of sin: death; A summary of these meditations.

— Fourth Meditation, The second effect of sin: the particular judgment.

— Fifth Meditation, The general judgment.

— Sixth Meditation, Hell.

— Seventh Meditation, The Council of the Trinity on the Incarnation; The principal circumstances of the life, passion and death of our Lord.

— Eighth Meditation, Spend the last two days on the Divine Attributes.

A.15 Conformity to the Divine Will

(c. 1632)[12]

Holy Communion with the Body of Jesus Christ causes us truly to participate in the joy of the Communion of Saints in Paradise. This joy was merited for us by the Incarnation and the death of the Son of God. So powerful was this merit, that the reconciliation of human nature by means of it is so great that we can never again be separated from the love of God. Just as God sees Himself united to man in heaven by the hypostatic union of the Word made Flesh, so He wanted such a union on earth so that the human race would never again be separated from Him.

O Infinite Love! Why do You allow blind creatures to neglect so great a good? This good can only be lost by sin which alone prevents the union between Your goodness and humanity. But, O my God, what is the cause of sin? It is self-love which, by the chaos it entails, prevents Your holy will from being fully accomplished. I hereby renounce self-love with all my heart and choose Your holy will as the directing force in my life. I shall recognize Your will by reflecting upon the life which Your Son led upon earth, to which I shall strive to conform my own. O Holy Will of my God! How reasonable it is that You should be completely fulfilled! You were the meat of the Son of God upon earth. Therefore, You are the nourishment which will sustain within my soul the life received from God. But what are You in the life of grace? You are grace itself which sanctifies souls . . . Thus, no more self-will! May Your will alone be the rule of my life! Grant me this grace, O my Jesus, for the love which You have for me and through the intercession of Your Holy Mother who loved so perfectly all the effects of Your loving will. I beg this grace of You, with all my heart and I give myself entirely to You, imploring Your goodness to overlook any contrary dispositions still to be found in me. I pray that the force of Your love, by its gentle power, may compel the acquiescence of any of my senses which may continue to oppose You.

To go to my new home with the motive of honoring Divine Providence which is leading me there. To place myself in the disposition to do all that this same Providence will permit to be accomplished there.

By this change of residence, to honor the changes made by Jesus and the Blessed Virgin when they moved from Bethlehem to Egypt and then to other places, not wanting, any more than they, to have a permanent dwelling here on earth.

May our love for God lead us to desire His glory and to sing His praise. Let us rejoice in His greatness, in all that He is in Himself, praising and loving His attributes and making acts of love as frequently as possible throughout the day.

1. What is grace? It is an act of the will. It is a gift to the soul that welcomes God. What is called light is nothing new. Rather, God, by a special grace, removes any obstacle that would prevent the soul from recognizing His gift.

2. What is it for God to perform a miracle any time at all? It is nothing new.

3. The soul must be attentive to supernatural graces which should not be called supernatural if . . .

A.5   (Retreat)

(c. 1632)

1. On the gravity of sin because of the sufferings our Lord endured to expiate it; *pride* and vain glory, a summary of my meditation.

On the infinite excellence of our Lord and on His call inviting men to follow Him.

2. On the openness necessary to hear the call of Jesus Christ and to renounce all things to follow Him; a summary of my meditation.

3. On the excellent way in which our Lord joins the contemplative to the active life; a summary of my meditation.

4. On the life of our Lord in Nazareth and the temptations to which He was subjected in the desert; a summary of my meditation.

5. On the evangelical counsels which our Lord set forth in the Sermon on the Mount; their excellence and the high perfection to which they call us; a summary of my meditation.

6. On the appearance of our Lord to all His disciples on the Mount of Galilee; the commands He gave them; the promises He made to them; summary of my meditation.

7. On the recollection and prayer of the Apostles between the Ascension and Pentecost as they prepared to receive the Holy Spirit; a summary of my meditation.

8. On the wonderful works which the Holy Spirit accomplished through the Apostles on Pentecost.

Our Lord desired to unite Himself so intimately to us by His love that God, His Father, punished in Him the enormity of sin. Nothing, therefore, can separate me from Jesus except sin which must now be punished in each person. To avoid it, I must unite myself closely to Jesus by imitating His most holy life.

Pride and all its effects are great obstacles to the action and plan of God in the soul. Since I recognize this to be true in my case, I shall strive to simplify the workings of my mind and to keep it humble not only in order to receive the grace of God, but also out of gratitude for His love because, in recommending this virtue, He did not teach us to practice it on account of our lowliness but in imitation of Him who is Himself humble of heart.

Willingly must I allow Jesus to take possession of

my soul and reign there as King. Thus, I shall preserve the joy I experience in realizing that each of us individually may desire and, indeed, has the power to become His well-beloved.

Because Jesus took our misery upon Himself, it is only reasonable that we should follow Him and imitate His holy, human life. This thought absorbed my mind and moved me to resolve to follow Him wholeheartedly, without any reservation. Filled with consolation and happiness at the thought of being accepted by Him to live my entire life as His follower, I resolved that in everything, particularly in uncertàin or questionable circumstances, I would consider what Jesus would have done and honor His submission to His Mother during the years when He was dependent upon her as her Son. Kneeling before the Blessed Sacrament, I felt interiorly moved to freely place myself in a disposition of total availability in order to receive the call of God and to carry out His most holy will. I considered that I was unworthy that the goodness of God should have a design for my soul. But I desired that it be fully accomplished in me and I offered my entire life to Him for this end.

I shall abandon myself completely into the hands of God in gratitude for His great love which led Him to manifest Himself to the whole human race and for the knowledge He gave His creatures of the means they have to give themselves entirely to Him.

All the actions and the entire life of the Son of God are only for our example and instruction . . . since He could have performed all of His miraculous works of and by Himself. This should give me great courage and confidence to undertake all that He will ask of me because, what I am unable to do on account of my powerlessness or other obstacles in me, God will do by His kindness and omnipotence.

41

Jesus grew before God by repeated acts of virtue. He grew before men as they gradually became aware of His excellent virtue. I shall honor this state by longing for an increase of the divine glory within me and by submitting, as far as possible, to creatures for love of Him.

The law of my God, as such, constitute an obligation for me and, with the help of His grace, I have resolved to practice it. But, the example of His dear Son, in the fulfillment of this law, instructs us and has moved me to resolve to assist my neighbor to understand it, insofar as I am able. Since I consider myself unworthy of such an undertaking, I can only offer myself completely to God that He might carry out this desire which does not come from me.

We have an evident proof of the love of God for us in the fact that He was pleased to teach us through the words of His Son that we must be perfect as He is perfect. This leads me to hope in His divine mercy. Since He is impeccable by nature, He will grant me the grace to reject sin. Therefore, I shall do all in my power to avoid it. Moreover, I hope that His divine goodness will allow me to share in those virtues which are essentially His. I shall implore this benefit not only for myself but also for all souls created for Him in order to honor the act by which God humbled Himself so as to raise up His creatures.

The humility of God who calls us to be perfect as He is perfect should give me great courage and lead me to great purity of intention. It should also make me confident that He will never fail to assist me when He asks something of me which is beyond my capabilities.

I must have great trust in God and believe that His grace will be sufficient to enable me to fulfill His holy will, however difficult it may appear to be, provided the Holy Spirit is truly calling me. I shall know this by listening to the advice which He will permit me to receive.

I shall honor the divine will by which the Holy Spirit led our Lord into the desert to be tempted. I shall do this, firstly, by calmly enduring the temptations of the devil and by repressing my pride which is wounded at its failure to recognize temptation disguised under the appearance of good. I shall honor this mystery, secondly, by a lively and trusting faith that the will of God for me will be accomplished, provided I allow myself to be led by Him.

I must imitate Jesus as a spouse tries to resemble her husband. Therefore, since to give me the greatest possible proof of His love, He chose the lowliest of surroundings, I accept the choice He wills me to make of the humblest possible way of life in a place where there is no worldly satisfaction.

The surest means of receiving the grace of God is to obey His holy inspirations as the Apostles did by going, as their Master had directed them, to the mountain where He appeared to them. I am struck by the charity of the Apostles who were not content with going there alone but who, by their example and preaching, brought a large crowd with them. As far as I am able, I must imitate this example and work for the salvation of my neighbor so that God may be glorified.

I shall greatly honor and respect those persons who hold the place of the Apostles since God has granted them the power to make us His children and to dispense His grace to us by means of the sacraments.

The recollection of the Apostles shall be an example for me to keep myself interiorly recollected by great and total dependence on the Providence of

God. Thus, closely united to God, I shall await the time when He shall be pleased to reveal what He is asking of me.

The principal reason for the recollection of the Apostles was their love for their Master. This same love must also be the sole reason for my dependence in which, with the help of His grace, I shall persevere all my life, ever longing for His love and hoping that, after having persistently begged for it in time, I may receive it in eternity.

I must perseveringly await the coming of the Holy Spirit although I do not know when that will be. I must accept this uncertainty as well as my inability to clearly perceive at this time the path which God wishes me to follow in His service. I must abandon myself entirely to His Providence so as to be completely His. In order to prepare my soul for this, I must willingly renounce all things to follow Him.

A.8 Retreat

(c. 1633)[13]

Saturday morning
The only means for me to find the mercy of God at the hour of my death is to have, at that moment, the image of Jesus Christ imprinted upon my soul. I must do this if I believe that His words are truly of God. I shall, therefore, have great confidence in Him who has assured me that, despite my misery and powerlessness, He will accomplish all that He desires in me. So as not to be taken by surprise by the uncertainty of the moment of death, I shall dispose myself to practice all that He asks of me.

One means to attain my goal is that, without there being anything in me to indicate it, others see me as having received graces from God. This humbles me but, at the same time, gives me courage.

No desires — no resolutions — The grace of my God will accomplish whatever He pleases in me.

Saturday: 10 o'clock

Since death is a necessary detachment from all things except the works which we have regularly produced, I shall strive to detach myself willingly and effectively from everything so as to truly and habitually attach myself to God. This practice alone may be called death since true physical death has been exalted by the death of Jesus Christ who transformed it for us into an entrance into life. I had the strong feeling that God was asking such a resolution of me after the example of our Lord who, during His life on earth, said that He had come to separate fathers from their children and, in general, to break all attachment to creatures.

Saturday: 2 o'clock

If I want to avoid the harsh and severe repudiation of Jesus, my Judge, I must live in such a way that my purity of intention, in all of my actions, will hide me from the eyes of the world so that I may be seen by God alone and ignored by the world and the devil. I wish to be ignored by the world because its praise is of no use to me and by the devil, so that, having disavowed me, he cannot accuse me.

I shall also have confidence in and devotion to my guardian angel so that he will assist me in this painful undertaking.

Sunday morning

Our Lord, born in poverty and obscurity, teaches me the purity of His love which He does not manifest to His creatures. He is satisfied simply to do whatever is necessary for them. Thus, I must learn to remain hidden in God, desiring to serve Him without seeking recognition from others or satisfaction in communicating with them, content that He sees what I am striving to become. To this end, He wants me to give myself to Him so that He can form this disposition in me. I did so with the help of His grace.

Sunday: 10 o'clock
I shall honor the serenity of the Crib by a disposition to replace desire by contentment in the possession of God who never denies Himself to the soul that truly seeks Him. I shall calmly adore the divinity in the Infant Jesus and imitate, to the best of my ability, His holy humanity, especially His simplicity and charity which led Him to come to us as a child so as to be more accessible to His creatures.

Sunday: 2 o'clock
The Crib is the throne of the Kingdom of Holy Poverty in which I ardently desire to be a subject, since the King of the Poor loved this virtue above all others. He proved this by allowing only the truly poor and simple to recognize Him. To this end, He revealed His birth by heavenly voices, thus assuring the listeners that God Himself honors this lowly state. In order to participate in this grace, I must, in imitation of the shepherds, correspond to the holy inspirations of God, without delay.

Sunday: 5 o'clock
I must be greatly ashamed on account of my pride and, in imitation of the Holy Virgin, humble myself not only when there is true reason to do so but I must

even give myself to God to serve my neighbor in situations where I will be subject to blame in the eyes of the world. Thus, I shall imitate our Lord who conversed with sinners and who, throughout His life, despised His own temporal interests so as to be useful to His creatures. I desire to do likewise if such be His holy will.

Monday morning
The Life of our Lord from the Age of Twelve until the Age of Thirty.
I must spend the rest of my days honoring the hidden life of Jesus on earth. He came among us to accomplish the will of God His Father. He did this during His entire life. Since He saw that the common life had the greatest need of examples, He devoted more time to it in the continual practice of evangelical perfection. He was rich but He chose holy poverty. He subjected Himself to the Blessed Virgin and to Saint Joseph by His obedience to them. I implore Him, with all my heart, to grant me the grace to imitate Him. Although I am unworthy, I hope that, after having filled me with this desire for so many years, He will, in His goodness, effectively bestow it upon me.

Second Meditation
I must bear in mind the fact that the humility which our Lord practiced at His Baptism is not only a source of humiliation for me but it must also serve as an example which I must imitate, neither to a greater nor to a lesser degree, than would an apprentice imitate his master if he wanted to become perfect. I should have no other thought, leaving the care of the rest to Divine Providence.

Nothing should keep me from humbling myself. For this, I have the example of our Lord who had a legitimate interest in advancing His glory and in reminding His Apostles of their obligation to honor Him, yet He did not shrink from humbling Himself to the point of washing the feet of His Apostles immediately before His passion.

At Holy Mass, as I was giving myself wholeheartedly to the Blessed Virgin so as to belong entirely to God according to His good pleasure, it seemed to me that our Lord was presenting my past and future unworthiness to His Holy Mother. Believing that they both had accepted me, I asked a proof that . . .

A.12   (Renunciation of Self)

(c. 1633)[14]

I must make good use of the advice which has been charitably given to me concerning the distinctions which appear among persons working together for the same goal, who have similar and nearly equal responsibilities for its outcome as well as those which exist when there is a single person responsible for the project who, through necessity, employs an assistant to direct it, who must be looked upon only as his representative. It seems to me that this is how I should consider myself in the tasks which God gives me. Therefore, I must submit, with no resistance whatever on my part, to the directives of those in power for the good of this work, although this was not apparent to me from the beginning!

On Easter Sunday, my meditation was on my desire to rise with our Lord. Since, without death, there can be no Resurrection, I realized that it was my evil inclinations which must die and that I must die completely to myself by deadening my passions and desires. I saw clearly that of myself I could never hope to achieve this, but it seemed to me that our good God was asking it of me. Therefore, I gave Him my full consent to operate in me by His power whatever He willed to see accomplished.

A.53   Notes on the Visits to the Confraternities[15] (Pont-Sainte-Maxence, Verneuil, Gournay Neufville and Bulles)

(1633)

I arrived in Verneuil and stayed at the home of a baker named La Caille. I saw two sick persons there, a man and a woman. The Ladies are responsible for different neighborhoods. There is only one where there are any sick; therefore the Ladies of the other neighborhoods do not visit. They only have the sacraments administered in cases of serious illness. They complain that the Treasurer is a difficult character who does not easily accept the advice of others. They tend to act according to their personal whim. They only bring food to the sick at eleven o'clock. The Superioress suggested not waiting until the sick had sold everything before caring for them.

They have some financial resources. Madame wants to buy a house to shelter the poor. Others suggested buying a few pieces of land because of the mortality rate of the livestock. There seems to be cordiality among the Ladies although some of them sometimes criticize the behavior of the Officers.

Linen — Bread — The Superioress wants to terminate the care of the sick too soon, according to the complaints of the Ladies. They do not meet to discuss the needs of the poor and they do not read their Rules. The Ladies go to the funeral Mass and to the cemetery when the men who are lodged in the house belonging to the Charity die.

I arrived in Pont on Tuesday and stayed at "The Fleur de Lys." The Ladies of Charity visit the sick except during times of plague, but they bring bouillon only at noon and leave very little. They give Holy Communion to the dying, prepare their bodies for burial and attend the funeral. They do not do anything more for the Ladies who die. They have funds but are afraid to invest them profitably for fear of diminishing alms. They have a sick call set to bring to the homes of the sick when they are to receive our Lord. They seek alms from the local residents and obtain four pounds or more each week.

I arrived in Gournay on Thursday. The Ladies are a little more coarse here than elsewhere, and there seems to be less charity among them. They have always had a few sick persons whom they often place in a private home in the care of a woman to whom they give five sous a day to look after them. However, they go to visit the sick three times a day and, since there are not many, they cook the meat in their own homes.

The litanies are said after Mass. They have no chapel, nor do they have a painting. They would like to have both. The people criticize them because they use alms to have Masses celebrated. There are some sick persons who have financial resources, but they can neither sell nor pawn anything because of the laws concerning the inheritance of widows. These persons are assisted from private alms, provided this is not a burden to the poor and there is a surplus. A painting— There are neither lambs nor sheep.

I arrived in Neufville-le-Roy, on Saturday at noon. I stayed at the inn. There are six sheep and six lambs and only about thirteen to fifteen pounds in revenue.

The peasants complain and the Ladies are prevented from doing what they should. When there is a sick person who has assets which he cannot sell because they are so tied up, I advised that he be told to bring in his creditors, who can authorize the sale and that, once he has paid them, he can live on the surplus. If his lands are covered with grain, he should sell before the harvest. If he has but one house he should sell it but retain the right to live in it for the remainder of his life.

There is much dissension among the Ladies over the reception of the sick and the purchase of meat. Each one wants to bring the meat from home according to her whim if she does not receive the customary amount. There is no High Mass on the first Sunday of the month and the litanies have only been sung once. The Ladies receive Holy Communion on almost all the appointed days.

On Monday, I arrived in Bulles where there were no sick. A Lady had died and the others had not received Holy Communion for her. Some of them do not receive Holy Communion each month. There has been some ill-feeling about collecting alms. The sick are visited three times a day and they are given the regular portion of cooked meat. However, the meat is not equally distributed to the sick because some of the Ladies want to bring home whatever they have left at the end of the day. There are fifteen or sixteen sheep and ten or twelve lambs being raised by local peasants for the benefit of the Charity. The first six they purchased died. They have pallets, bolsters, mattresses, blankets and a lot of linen as well as about forty-five pounds. They have a vigil, a High Mass and a funeral Mass offered for the Ladies who die, but the people complain about this.

A.52 Visits to the Confraternities of Verneuil, Pont-Sainte-Maxence, Gournay, Neufville and Bulles (1633)[16]

There have almost always been sick persons to care for in Verneuil since the establishment of the Charity. However, because the village is very spread out, the Ladies complain that only the Ladies from one neighborhood actually visit and they asked that the custom of dividing the village into neighborhoods for service be abandoned.

The Treasurer, on account of her ill-health, does nothing more than keep the money. She is not on good terms with the other officers and she is sometimes difficult to deal with, even in receiving and discharging the sick who, because they are let go too soon after recovering their health, sometimes have a relapse.

The Superioress suggested that they not wait until the sick have sold everything before assisting them. The Ladies complained that the officer in charge of the goods of the Charity put new shirts and sheets into daily use. They seem fairly cordial with one another and have a deep affection for the Charity.

The poor are served every day as the Rule ordains but the portion of meat is only brought at eleven o'clock. They have some financial resources. The Marquise wants the Charity to buy a house to shelter the sick while some other Ladies want to purchase a small piece of land because of the loss of livestock which sometimes occurs. The Superioress complained that many of those who had promised thread are no longer willing to give it. The sick receive the sacraments only when they are seriously ill.

Nearly all the Ladies receive Holy Communion on the appointed days but they do not meet to discuss the needs of the poor nor do they read their Rules.

They attend the funeral Mass and go to the cemetery when a member dies and they do the same for others who have requested it, although they do not belong to the Confraternity, when they have left a donation to the Charity.

In Pont-Sainte-Maxence, the Ladies of Charity faithfully visit the sick except during time of plague when they assist the poor with the money of the Charity because the city abandons them. They even gave six sheets to a person who was caring for these poor victims because they discovered that she had nothing but straw.

When they visit, the Ladies bring the portions of meat already cooked, but they only do so at noon and they leave only a little bouillon. They prepare the dead for burial, attend the funeral, and offer their next Holy Communion for them. They attended the funeral of the first Lady of the Confraternity and showed signs of grief. They received Holy Communion for her and accompanied the body to the cemetery.

This Charity is well supplied. They even have a sick call set which they bring to the homes of the sick who are to receive our Lord. They show great cordiality to one another and are devoted to works of charity. Even their husbands encourage them in their endeavors. The people have noticed them, and since the establishment of the Charity, the local inhabitants are better. The Treasurer has funds which she is afraid to invest profitably for fear of diminishing revenues. Requests for donations are made in the homes of the local residents.

In Gournay, there have been sick to be cared for since the foundation of the Charity. They are visited three times a day. Each Lady cooks the allotted portions of meat in her own home.

The local inhabitants complain that charitable donations are used to have Masses said. The Ladies are prevented from doing what they ought when they find sick persons who have property which they cannot sell and are thus ineligible for assistance. The Charity has not cared for these poor sick who must be assisted by charitable individuals. The Ladies here are somewhat lacking in refinement and are less united among themselves than elsewhere.

They have neither an altar nor a painting but they would like to have both. Mass is celebrated every month, followed by the litanies. Many receive Holy Communion at this time. The sick who are without shelter are housed with a woman who cares for them for five sous a day. This expenditure is necessary because they have neither sheep nor lambs and very little money.

In Neufville, the peasants complain because the sick are not attended to quickly enough. The officers are prevented from doing what they should for the sick who have assets which they cannot sell. There is some dissension among the Ladies because they want to know everything that is going on and give their advice on it. There are also disputes because, on their appointed days, they each want to bring what suits their fancy to the sick and take from their own homes things which have not been given to them. There are six sheep and six lambs which are undernourished. They have about fifteen or sixteen pounds in the treasury. The sick are visited three times a day. The Ladies usually receive Holy Communion on the appointed days. The Mass on the first Sunday of the month is not a High Mass, but the Pastor says that the Bishop of Beauvais does not want it to be. The litanies have only been sung once.

There was a sick woman who had property which she gave in its entirety to her relatives before or during her illness without the knowledge of the Ladies, who now wonder if they should serve such persons under these circumstances since the timing of the gift may have been deliberate.

The sick poor of Bulles are visited three times a day. They bring cooked portions of meat but not in equal amounts to all because each Lady wants to take from her home what she judges right so as to please the sick.

Many of the Ladies do not receive Holy Communion for months at a time. A member died and they did not receive Holy Communion for her. However, they did attend the funeral and had a vigil and a complete funeral service celebrated. The people complained about this.

There are often little disputes among the Ladies which interfere with their practice of charity. Some of them do not wish to be in the company of those with whom they have quarreled. The Superioress is sometimes able to remedy the situation.

There are pallets, mattresses, bolsters, blankets and an abundance of linen. There are also fifteen or sixteen sheep and ten or twelve lambs which are raised by local peasants for the benefit of the Charity. The first six that they had purchased died, so they had to buy others. There are about forty-five pounds in the treasury. The Procurator administers everything with great charity. He is well respected and loved.

The Ladies would like to have some medals since none of them have any. The possibility of gaining indulgences would move them to receive Holy Communion more often.

A.43 On the Good Use of Suffering

I experienced consolation in my great sorrow without feeling that it was for the love of God. Therefore, desiring to make good use of my weakness and recognizing my powerlessness, I recalled the suffering of another person and united my intention to his and offered them to God with our Lord on the Cross.

On the Feast of Saint Bernard, after Holy Communion, regretting my little knowledge and love of God which caused me to fill my mind with so much that was not of Him, I had the firm desire to concentrate all my thoughts on God as the only means to rid my mind of other things. I continued in this state since I wanted to be instructed on the means I should employ.

A.35 Prayer to a Patron Saint of France

Complete the work which our loving God has given you to do. You know the greatness of the mysteries which Jesus has left us in order to sanctify souls born of His blood in His Spouse, the Church. Help them, therefore, to esteem their calling and guide them by your prayers.

Blessed state of the Christian which makes the soul no less than an associate of God.

Let the souls that you possess feel your possession. But, possess them with gentle power, leading them to live as their state requires, aware that pride of the senses no longer has any place in their lives nor does resistance to the omnipotence of God who wishes to share His joy with them.

O Great Saint, your interest and the glory of God oblige you to pray for France. It is well that she still needs your powerful assistance to draw her once again from malicious idolatry rather than from ignorance. Watch over the clergy who are extending their hands to you for help as to another Elisha pleading for your twofold spirit so as to better understand hidden mysteries. You see how greatly God has been dishonored by them from whom He should receive glory because of the priestly character which has consecrated them and totally dedicated them to the service of the altar where He is to be adored.

Period Between 1633 and 1647

A.55 Order of the Day
(Observed by the First Daughters of Charity)

(1633)

They shall rise at five-thirty and kneel down beside their beds to adore God and to ask His blessing so that they may employ the day in keeping with His most holy will.

They shall dress, make their beds and, at six o'clock, they shall go to the oratory to make their meditation.

They shall conclude their meditation at seven o'clock after which they shall say the Litany of the Blessed Virgin, the Respice, the Retribuere, the De Profundis, and the Prayer to the Guardian Angel.

They shall then give an account of their prayer and shall carefully remember their most important resolutions so as to practice them during the day.

Those who are to serve the sick on that day shall go to the home of the Lady who is cooking the food to see that all will be ready to begin distribution at nine-thirty.

Those who are in charge of the medicines shall distribute them after prayers. Upon their return, they shall go to Mass.

After Mass, they shall learn to read or they shall do their work.

At noon, they shall make the particular examen on the way they have practiced the resolutions made during meditation. They shall say the Benedicite and then they shall dine.

After Grace, without kneeling, they shall recall their good resolutions and ask God for the strength to practice them for the remainder of the day.

Those who are in charge of the medicines shall go to the doctor for the prescriptions and attend to whatever is most pressing. Those who take food to the sick shall contact the Lady who will prepare it the next day.

When they have all returned to the house, they shall continue their work, study, and then after repeating the principal points of their faith in the form of a short catechism, they shall read a passage of the Holy Gospel so as to stimulate themselves to the practice of virtue and the service of their neighbor in imitation of the Son of God.

Those who serve the sick keep a constant watch on their needs such as wood, linen, preserves, infusions, and other necessities.

At six o'clock, they shall take their reading after which they shall make the particular examen on the manner in which they have practiced their good resolutions. They shall say the Benedicite and then have supper after which they shall say Grace.

After supper, they shall have recreation; then they shall give an account of what they remember from the reading. Anyone who wishes to do this privately may do so.

They shall continue their work until nine o'clock at which time they shall make the general examen and then recite aloud the Confiteor, the Misereatur, the Indulgentiam, the Visita quaesumus, the Respice, the Angelus, the Retribuere, the De Profundis and the Litany of Jesus. They shall go to bed at ten o'clock after kneeling down beside their beds to adore God and to ask His blessing for the night.

They shall be disposed to receive Holy Communion on some feasts and Sundays. However, they shall remember not to ask this permission of their confessor without informing me. I shall use this occasion to remind them of some faults which should not be found in persons who communicate frequently.

A.54 Draft of the Rule[17]

The Confraternity of widows and village girls has been instituted to honor our Lord, its patron, and the Blessed Virgin, and to imitate, in some way, the women and young girls of the Gospel who followed and ministered to our Lord and His Apostles. While doing this, they shall work at their own perfection, for the salvation of their families, and for the corporal and spiritual assistance of the sick poor of this city and of the country, whom they shall serve themselves in their parishes and for whom they shall procure the able assistance of the Ladies of Charity in the villages. They shall provide funds from their common purse for the village Charities which would otherwise be unable to care for the poor and they shall see to it that all involved do their best to enable the poor who recover to lead a good life for the rest of their days and those who die to leave this world in a good state.

The said Confraternity shall be directed by three of the widows or older girls, who shall be elected for three years by a majority vote of the membership. The votes shall be tabulated by the Superior of the Mission or his delegate. One of those elected shall be the Superioress, another the Treasurer, and another the Procuratrix.

The Superioress shall see to it that the present Rules are observed; assume the *direction of the widows*[18] insofar as the Confraternity is concerned; *receive into the Confraternity*[19] those village girls whom she judges suitable and dismiss those who, in her opinion, do not possess the required qualities. She shall also transfer these village girls from one place to another; direct them in the ways of salvation; teach them to take good care of the sick poor, in keeping with the end of the Company, and to instruct country children. She shall also correct them.

In a word, the Superioress shall be the soul which animates the body and which enables it to carry out the plan of God for it. Nevertheless, she shall fulfill her responsibilities under the direction of the Priest of the Mission appointed by the Superior and in consultation with the two officers when they reside in the House. When they are at a distance, she shall seek their advice only in very important matters.

The Treasurer shall serve as a councillor to the Superioress. In this capacity, she shall keep a register of the receipts and expenditures. She shall retain in her possession the key to the safe in which are kept the papers and money of the Confraternity except the three hundred pounds which remain in the hands of the Procuratrix. She shall give a financial report once a year to the officers in the presence of the above named Superior.

The Procuratrix shall also serve as a councillor to the Superioress as the need arises and, with the approval of the said Superioress, she shall see to it that provisions are not lacking and that the one who replaces her in the House when she is not in residence there carefully carries out this responsibility. She shall give a report on the same day as the Treasurer.

The above mentioned widows shall look upon the Superioress in our Lord and our Lord in her. They are obliged to observe the Rules of this House and those who reside elsewhere must obey the Rule drawn up for them. They shall contribute to the support of this good work, in keeping with their means and their devotion. They shall cherish one another as Sisters whom our Lord has united by the bond of His love. They shall love the girls as the handmaids of Jesus

Christ. They shall meet at least once a month to discuss the matters contained in their Rule.

Once a year, the said widows shall make a spiritual retreat. They shall go to the Motherhouse for this purpose. Insofar as they are able, they shall visit the Confraternities of Charity in the country districts when asked to do so by the Superioress and always in keeping with the directive of the Superior of the Mission or of the priests appointed by him.

The girls shall look upon the widows as their Mistresses and their Mothers. They shall honor the Blessed Virgin whom they shall see in them. They shall obey their Superioress, looking upon our Lord in her and her in our Lord. They shall cheerfully go wherever they are sent, either to the city or to the country, and they shall return in the same spirit whenever they are recalled by the Superioress. They shall serve the sick poor and they shall show the Ladies of the Charity of the place where they are sent *the manner in which this care is to be provided.* They shall teach them how to prepare and distribute medicines and how to treat wounds and other ailments. As far as possible they shall only leave their rooms, two by two, to go to Church, to obtain provisions, and to visit the sick in their lodgings. They shall never stop to speak with anyone on the way. They shall teach the little girls of the villages while they are there. They shall strive to train local girls to replace them at this task during their absence. They shall do all this for the love of God and without any remuneration.

A.47   Visit to the Confraternity of Gournay

(1636)

There should be a large register containing the establishment and Rule of the Charity, the names of the members, the election of the first and second Officers, the election of the second Procurator and, finally, the following information:

On the Feast of the Blessed Trinity, May 18, 1636, the Ladies of the Charity assembled at the Château, in the presence of Madame de Gournay, to discuss the affairs of the said Company, for the service of the poor. During the meeting, they resolved once again to practice their Rule exactly and to proceed to the election of Officers, as is prescribed, with no preferences and so as to avoid a misunderstanding of the past which had led them consistently to place officers in different responsibilities and to change them. They resolved that next year the Treasurer and the Officer responsible for the goods of the Confraternity should remain in office for the following year while the other two would be replaced so that, subsequently, each year those who had held office for two years would be changed. A majority vote of the membership shall determine which two officers are to remain.

They also resolved that they would each carry a candle in the procession which takes place every third Sunday after Vespers and that, as far as possible, they would accompany the Blessed Sacrament to and from the homes of the sick.

On this same day, Madame de Gournay asked to be received into the Company of Charity and she was accepted. The widow of the deceased . . . also asked to be admitted. Since Madame . . . had relinquished her place because she was moving to Paris, it was decided that she would be received after she had lived in Gournay for three months and had assured the members that she was determined to remain there at least for the lifetime of her husband.

The Ladies of the Charity asked two questions. They wanted to know, first, if it were necessary to wait until the sick had entirely disposed of all their assets before they could be accepted for care by the Charity and, second, if a non-resident of the village should fall ill, should he be cared for by them.

It was decided that if the sick had extra furnishings or clothing, such as pewter dishes and the like, or wine or a little wheat or even a bread oven, all had to be sold before they could be assisted. However, should they have a piece of land from which they can derive no profit, they should be accepted for care by the Charity. Such would not be the case, if they have an acre to which they have clear title.

They also asked if they could assist those sick persons who would want to give their few assets to the Charity after their death or their cure so as to repay the expenses incurred in caring for them. They were told that they should not do so because they are obliged to serve the poor with no thought of remuneration. Moreover, by so doing, they would place themselves in danger of losing what had been given to them or of becoming involved in a lawsuit, which must be avoided at all cost. However, should it happen that a sick person whom they have assisted, desires, at the hour of death, to leave property to the Charity, they may accept it, provided the sick person has not been asked to do this by the Ladies; does not have any debts; and does not have any heirs in need.

In another part of the register, they should record the deaths of the Ladies.

In yet another section, there should be a record of the sick who have been accepted for care and the date on which they were discharged either because they were cured or had died. Finally, there should be a section for the extraordinary donations made to the Charity along with the necessary legal documents and a listing of the belongings of the sick. This book is never to be removed from the safe!

A.77 Practices Which Our Sisters Should Observe When Traveling to Their Little Foundations[20]

When they receive their Obedience, they shall give themselves to God to carry it out, asking for the grace to be faithful to Him in all things.

On the day of departure, they shall receive Holy Communion, if they can do so without too much difficulty. Then, after receiving the blessing of their Superior, they shall reflect that when they are traveling they are to honor the journeys of our Lord and strive to maintain a disposition of humble confidence in Divine Providence.

Their veil shall be modesty in their glances, words, and actions. They should be well aware that everyone in the coach will be observing their slightest movements. Therefore, they must be a source of edification rather than scandal.

They shall try to sit together in the coach so as to be able to hear one another and to discourage the other travelers from conversing with an individual sister.

When the coach leaves very early in the morning and they have not had time to make their meditation at the inn, they shall do so as soon as they are in the coach and have said the prayer for travelers. They shall continue their spiritual exercises on about the same schedule as at home.

When they pass through a village where the coach does not stop, they shall adore the Blessed Sacrament and greet the guardian angels of all the souls in this place.

They shall not eat at the guest table of the inn. As soon as they have arrived, they shall go to the nearest church to adore the Blessed Sacrament. Should there be any poor nearby, they shall visit them. Otherwise, they shall catechize those whom they meet. They shall eat together in some private place in the inn, having bought what was necessary the night before.

They shall eat at the usual time and observe the same frugality at meals as they do at home. If their zeal moves them to say a few good words to those around them, they shall be careful to do so humbly and modestly, avoiding all complacency.

In the evening, if it is not too late, they shall go to adore the Blessed Sacrament. They shall also give a few minutes instruction to the poor and distribute some holy cards. They shall do the same for the servants at the inn who often need to be instructed in things necessary for their salvation.

When they arrive, they shall ask the innkeeper's wife to provide them with a small room so that they can sleep separately from the others. They shall also eat there, practicing frugality because of the close quarters and in order to save something for the next day. Since bread is usually more expensive at an inn, they would be well advised to buy a good quantity from a baker so as to meet their needs.

They shall do their utmost to assist at Mass every day, but especially on Sundays and feast days. To this end, they shall inquire the night before the time of the first Mass the next day. If possible, on the eve of a feast, they shall go to confession so as to be able to receive Holy Communion. However, they shall be careful not to inconvenience their fellow travelers nor to miss the coach. Consequently, they shall try not to get separated from their companions.

A.21b   Meditations[21]

I desired to satisfy my obligations to the Eternal Father by offering Him the death of His Son, but I suddenly realized that this would be temerity and an offense against Him who, out of His goodness alone, had consented to the mystery of the Incarnation.

The Holy Communion of Eastertime is the only one commanded by the Church, which tells us thereby that its children will receive their inheritance from its Spouse today. This seemed to me to be a treasure capable of providing me with anything I might need throughout the year. This obliges us to chose the life of Jesus Crucified as the model for our lives so that His Resurrection may be a means for glory for us in Eternity. In order to live in this way, I thought that I must often reflect on His example. Therefore, I determined to make three or four acts each day, one in the morning, one at noon, and one in the evening, in which I would address myself to the holy humanity of our Lord, to the Blessed Virgin and to my guardian angel in order to abandon myself to the plan of God, to honor the life of the Word, and to ask for the spirit of steadfastness and counsel.

On March 2, when I received the news concerning our Sisters at Nanteuil, I recognized the fact that I had been unfaithful to God in allowing myself to be overwhelmed by these painful circumstances and in rushing off to seek a solution from those who could provide one rather than having recourse to God as I had resolved to do.

On the octave of the Feast of Corpus Christi, I adored the Blessed Sacrament in the chapel of our venerable Fathers. I begged our Lord, by the loving union of the Word with man, that both communities might be eternally united to Him; that we might remain forever united to the Roman Apostolic Hierarchy by means of the close union of each member of our communities with the poor, in conformity to the will of God. I had the thought, which I resolved to put into practice, of giving a painting of the Blessed Virgin, with the sun in the background to represent her Immaculate Conception, to the Cathedral of Chartres, to Saint-Lazare and to our motherhouse in order to obtain the preservation of the purity of both Companies. I asked this of God by the purity of His Incarnation.

This resolution has been carried out. I sent a small picture of Our Lady to Chartres; a small painting of the Blessed Virgin holding a pearl rosary to Saint-Lazare; and a wooden statue of Mary holding a chaplet of nine beads in honor of the nine months which Our Lord spent in her womb to the Motherhouse.

M.41 On the Sufferings of Purgatory

I reflected on the sufferings reserved after death for the person whom we might believe had lived at least for a few years without commiting mortal sin. I recall hearing that there was punishment in Purgatory to erase the guilt of the sinner who had failed to love and to desire to see God. I seemed to see the powers of the soul acting on his senses and passions, causing him to suffer from the excessive desire for satisfaction: his eyes to see; his ears to hear; his taste to savor; his nose to smell; his affectivity to love God and to hate himself.

A.16 Desire for Holy Communion

On the Feast of Saint Benedict, I had yet another reason for abandoning myself entirely to Divine Providence. After having failed to receive Holy Communion and grieving for my sins, I was moved by a strong desire for the Holy Eucharist. Therefore, I asked God that, if such be His holy will, He might inspire my confessor with this thought. I had said nothing to him about my desire when he sent for me to speak to me about it. I was greatly consoled by this very special grace of Divine Providence. In His goodness, God had revealed His great love for me by making me realize that, although I had forgotten some sins in confession and knew full well that sin alone could separate me from Him, His love was so great that not even sin could prevent Him from coming to me.

A.30 (Meditation on the Hunger and Thirst for Justice)

"Blessed are they who . . ." Hunger and thirst are two urgent needs of nature, especially in strong bodies. If our souls are healthy, they should have the same urges, not as passions, but as desires for justice.

It seems to me that justice consists of the general renunciation of all my passions which are so contrary to the commandments of God and to the perfection that He expects of me, as well as that charity which in words, actions and attitudes I am obliged to render to my neighbor.

Thirst for justice, which is a more pressing need, must lead us to desire greater things. We must long for union with God and the disposition and means to attain it. We must ardently desire that the effects of His holy will reign in us; and we must do all in our power to bring about this reign in others. It is only just that the owner should dispose as he sees fit of what is his without encountering any resistance. To attain this goal in my own life, I shall abandon myself entirely to Divine Providence and no longer seek to be the proprietor of my free will. Rather, I shall place myself in the hands of God and of my Superior. To put this resolution into effect, I shall gladly accept whatever God permits to happen to me, whether it comes directly from Him or through the instrumentality of His creatures, to whose judgment I shall acquiesce despite my repugnance to do so.

A.22 (On the Feast of the Blessed Trinity)

I desired to honor the Feast of the Blessed Trinity, as God has ordained that we should celebrate the Sabbath which is called the day of rest of the Lord, after the six days of the creation of the world. I thought that man is the chief work of God's creative power and that sin had, in a way, nullified this work by preventing the creature from rejoicing in His God. However, in His divine plan, God did not intend this separation to be permanent. Therefore, this same God, Father, Son and Holy Spirit, who had said, "Let us make man to our image and likeness," now resolved to create him anew by redeeming him. Since, after all the other mysteries of our Redemption, the Holy Spirit has inspired the Church to institute the Feast of the Blessed Trinity, it seems to me that God wills it to be solemnized as the day of rest.

M.35b (Dream, Eve of December 8)

On the vigil of the Feast of the Immaculate Conception of the Blessed Virgin, after I had heard the reading of the Epistle for this day, I saw, in a dream, a great darkness at noonday. It appeared insignificant at first but was followed by a black night which astounded and frightened everyone. I felt only submission to Divine Justice. Once the darkness had disappeared, I saw the radiance of the dawning day and, somewhere in the high heavens, a figure resembling the one presented to us in the Gospel of the Transfiguration but it seemed to be a woman. Nevertheless, I was filled with great astonishment and gratitude to God to such a degree that my body felt pain and I awoke. I continued to suffer for a time after that. Unlike my other dreams, this one has always remained in my mind as a representation of the first grace of the Blessed Virgin who is the beginning of the light which the Son of God was to bring to the world.

In my meditation on the subject of the Epistle, I saw that Holy Church applied *Being* to the Blessed Virgin before the Creation of the world. I accepted this concept, reflecting that not only was she in the mind of God from all eternity by His foreknowledge of her, but that she was there also in preference to all other creatures because of the dignity for which God had destined her as the Mother of His Son. He was able to so will it before the creation of all earthly things which would witness the sin of our fathers. God chose to accomplish an act of His own will for the creation of the soul of Mary. This could also have been an effective act. However, I am entirely submissive to the Church in this matter. I make use of these ideas only to give greater honor to the Holy Virgin and to renew the total dependence of the Company upon her as her most unworthy daughters, who look on her also as our most praiseworthy and only Mother.

May Jesus and Mary be loved!

A.32b   (Thought on the Blessed Virgin)

Prostrate yourself[22] before the Holy Virgin whom God willed to redeem before He created her. Reveal your conscience to her and ask her to obtain for you conversion of life, deliverance from your most urgent needs as well as a greater love for her Son and closer union with His divine humanity.

A.45b   (On the Feast of the Epiphany)

It is not enough to have a mind enlightened by the consciousness of our faults. Our wills must also be moved to correct them. In the first case we purify our conscience, while in the second we embellish and adorn it for the reception of our Jesus.

The cleansing is effected by the complete confession of all our sins; the embellishment by the practice of virtue, especially prayer, fasting and almsgiving which are, in a way, to people in the world, what the three vows of religion are to religious, i.e. almsgiving for poverty, fasting for chastity and prayer for obedience. We may also offer them at the Crib in place of the gifts of the Three Kings: almsgiving for gold, fasting for myrrh, and prayer for incense. Likewise, we may present them to the Blessed Trinity: prayer to the Father, fasting to the Son, and almsgiving to the Holy Spirit. Thus we are able to adore our Incarnate God with the angels by prayer, with the Kings by almsgiving, and with the shepherds by fasting; and God will bless us.

A.80   Rule for the Sisters Who Care for Children
(c. 1640)[23]

In the morning, as the sisters enter the children's room, they shall kneel in order to offer to God all the services that they are going to render to the childhood of Our Lord in the person of His children. They shall say the *Veni Sancte Spiritus,* and then sprinkle all the children with holy water, having them raise their hearts to God.

They shall have the children make acts of adoration, love, thanksgiving and supplication so as to avoid offending God during the day and throughout their lives.

Afterward, they shall have the girls who are with them get the children up and dressed properly.

As soon as they are dressed, the sisters shall have them kneel and pray to God by reciting acts of love of God, of adoration, and of thanksgiving.

Then, the children shall be given breakfast. The youngest, from three to four years old, shall receive some soup which has been simmered. The older children, the five, six, seven, and eight year olds, shall be given a piece of dry bread.

At ten o'clock, after having had them say the Benedicite, the sisters shall take care to have the children seated on their benches at their tables for dinner. At the end of dinner, they shall have them say Grace.

At one o'clock, the oldest children shall be assembled so that they may be taught catechism and their letters. After this, they shall be given a piece of bread with some sweets, if they are available.

At four o'clock, supper shall be prepared for the children.

At five o'clock, the sisters shall start putting the little ones to bed, and they shall have the older boys and girls pray to God. They are all to be in bed at six o'clock since they get up at five o'clock both winter and summer.

Once the children are in bed, the sisters shall take care to have them give their hearts once more to God, and sprinkle them with holy water as they did in the morning.

A.76   On Several Customs of the Motherhouse
(To obtain a decision from Vincent de Paul)
(after 1641)[24]

The rising bell rings at four o'clock. At four-thirty a bell rings for entrance into the chapel and the beginning of meditation.

The bell rings at eleven-thirty for dinner. Three strokes of the bell mark the rising from table.

The Vespers bell of Saint-Lazare serves to announce reading and silence. Instruction follows until three o'clock.

At five-thirty, the bell rings for the evening meditation. It rings for supper at six o'clock. Around six-fifteen, it is sounded as at dinner to mark the rising from table.

At eight o'clock, the bell rings for the reading of the *Martyrology.* The subject of meditation is given at this time and several sisters share their reflections until the quarter hour rings for all to go to the chapel for prayer.

We would like to have the Angelus rung three times a day.

It might be appropriate to have the readings and prayers done by different sisters, most often by the three Officers and sometimes by others, as is the custom of all communities for the Office and readings.

Perhaps the text, "the Sister Assistant will have the same power" includes authority over other Officers. This could be detrimental and could cause her to act imperiously. Such is already the case, although it has not been made public since there has not been a single protest. The sister in question was very careful to act in such a way that she maintains authority and credibility with the other sisters. It is for this reason, along with the others proposed, that the first two Sister Officers are each to give the instruction during their assigned week. This seems necessary for the Company. This has begun, but is not continuing with great regularity while we await orders in this matter.

Not being able to obtain the advice of the Sister Officers, particularly on the frequent changing of the sisters — quite a long period of reflection is needed on this, and on the situation. Then the necessity to change a sister quickly in order to send one who is, in reality, better suited.

A.91   Observations on the Rules
(First Notebook)[25]

It seems that the difficulty of keeping three reliable and capable sisters at the Motherhouse — two Officers would suffice — was not in training a new sister who would be responsible only for writing down the expenditures, nor was it in giving advice and counsel. The difficulty was in knowing whether there would be something to add to the article.

The first Officer and the appointed second Officer should not be called Sister Servant for the reasons given to Father Portail.

In the matter of the Treasurer, it would be better to put three hundred pounds instead of one hundred. This should be done in order to avoid confusion during the times when it is necessary to make an extraordinarily large expenditure, which too often requires searching through the safe.

The third Officer presents her accounts to the Treasurer every week. The Treasurer reports to the Superioress once a month. This is all either of them can do because of their many responsibilities.

(Second Notebook)

The third intention of the act of adoration commemorating the moment of our Lord's death is for the souls in Purgatory so that divine merit may be applied to them.

In the article on the evening examen, which concerns the account given of the reading or meditation, add that this is done after the reading of the *Martyrology*, provided there is enough time before the quarter hour rings.

The Friday Conferences are held only after evening prayer.

Catechism is held after Vespers on Sundays and feast days. The instruction spoken of in this article remains at the time indicated.

The seventeenth Article of this notebook is useless, there never having been any weaned children at the Motherhouse.

Common Rules

To explain or do away with the title of Sister Servant in an article.

To the article which speaks of the sisters first submitting their written letters to the Superioress shall also be added, "those letters which they receive." These are of greater concern.

In the article which says that all the sisters must be warned of their faults, should it not specify that the Officers must do it with equal exactitude and necessity?

The repetition of the Employment of the Day is cumbersome. It seems that it would suffice to state it once only and then to specify all the things particular to the parishes. We shall do this if we are ordered to do so and if it is necessary.

The custom is that the sisters make their request for Holy Communion to the Superioress at the Motherhouse. In other places, the request is made to the Sister Servant. This exercise in humility seems useful, provided that it is used well by both parties.

This is not spoken of in the chapter regulating the reception of Holy Communion.

For the sisters working with the foundlings
The article following the first one which deals with the spiritual service that the sisters give to the children is not to be on the subject of imitation of the Blessed Virgin. A few words of explanation seem necessary here. If the above is the case, it would be possible to add an article on the esteem that Our Lord has for the service which is rendered to children.

The Sister Servant must take care to point out to the Lady Treasurer of the Children the necessity of placing the children, particularly the boys, as soon as she sees that they are ready for domestic service or to learn a trade. She should try to recognize their inclinations and desires without their noticing it. She should especially do this for the boys so that they not be kept at the Motherhouse past the age of twelve. In this matter as in all others, she shall consult the Superioress of the Company of the Daughters of Charity before making a decision. Such collaboration will lead to great union between them. Thus, it would be necessary to amend the article which speaks of sixteen as the age at which boys must leave, unless it is the case of some crippled boy. Nevertheless, if a boy is judged to be causing harm to the other children because of some bad inclinations, the Sister Servant shall point it out so that the Ladies may have him placed in another hospital for the poor where he will cause no harm.

Should not the sister representing the Sister Servant be named her Assistant by Superiors? It will not be possible for this sister to have sole care of the weaned children; that would require another sister. This article would be more intelligible if it were written as two articles.

Should not the following article address itself to the Sister Servant in order to speak of her once again?

It seems to me that the following article, which speaks of the older children, is sufficiently covered in another article. This other article should be amended so that neither seems a repetition of the other.

In the article which speaks of neither adding nor subtracting anything, it would be necessary to specify which Superioress, since it could be understood that it is the Superioress of the Company of Ladies to which reference is being made. On this subject, I had remarked something similar to that, which probably will not be necessary.

The next to the last article should be divided into two separate articles.

Hôtel-Dieu[26]

If the sisters notice some extraordinary spiritual or temporal need in one of the sick poor, the Sister Servant shall give instructions on the matter to one of the Ladies.

Revise the article which speaks of having the children baptized. The sisters should no longer have them baptized in the hospital unless they have an extraordinary need for it.

The sisters should not communicate with nor receive anything from religious. Nor should they communicate with surgeons or apothocaries. It is to be ascertained whether or not Monsieur Vincent judges it appropriate for the sisters to ask the religious for remedies when they are ill or to give them freely to such religious. This began a few years ago without our knowledge, and the sisters even summoned surgeons to have them let their blood. I have prevented this for some time. However, I would like to propose easier access to remedies for the sisters.

Not to speak in the article concerning weaned children of following the custom of the Motherhouse, since they are not kept there.

In the last article, instead of saying, "The sister shall have the children brought", say "She will bring it to the attention of the Sister Servant of the hospital to send someone to bring the children to the hospital."

There should be an article speaking of the works of the house, as in the case of the parishes.

The Sister Servant shall be careful to write down the names of the Ladies who bring money to her. She shall also record the date and the sum which she receives so that she may give an account to the Lady Treasurer of the Hospital.

So long as there are collection boxes at Notre-Dame for the devastated provinces, or should they be left there later on for the children, and the sisters have keys for them, they shall be careful to empty the boxes at least once a week and every evening on great feast days. They shall keep a record of the funds collected in order to deposit this money with the Lady in charge of this matter.

The sisters of the parishes

To this article should be added the respect and obedience that the sisters owe the Ladies and the doctor. The doctor shall be dealt with with great reserve, as is the confessor of the poor.

The sisters must have care to encourage the sick to receive the sacraments, doing their utmost to help them prepare themselves well for this. The sisters must also procure consolation for the sick when they are in true need of it, respecting them and speaking to them gently and humbly never thinking that the poor owe them anything for these services.

The sisters should pay no more attention to the praise given by the poor than to their insults and contempt, except to try to make good use of them—

refusing the praise interiorly and welcoming the insults in order to honor the contempt shown the Son of God.

An article should state that the sisters must make the beds when necessary and that the Sister Servant should know of it. Another article should state that the sisters must be diligent in all that they do, and that they must work even if there is not sufficient work to be done for the poor. If there is no work to be done, the sisters should ask for it from the Motherhouse, as has been the case for some time.

Several of these items are included in the Common Rules. However, since these things apply particularly to them, it will be more useful to treat of them all here.

For the sisters employed with galley slaves

It should be included in one of the articles that the sisters shall not argue with the galley slaves, even to help them to understand the reasons for the unpleasantness which they claim to have been caused by the sisters. Also, the sisters must never reproach them nor speak rudely to them. Moreover, the galley slaves should be treated with great compassion, as much for their spiritual state as for their most pitiful corporal state.

The sisters must never speak to any one galley slave in particular, nor give credence to them when they try to justify their crimes. Likewise, the sisters must turn a deaf ear toward their pleas for help in escaping their predicament because of the evil which it entails.

In order to make it intelligible, changes should be made in the article which instructs the sisters to seek advice on the galley slaves' temporal welfare from the Sister Servant.

When some extraordinary expenditure is to be made for the galley slaves by one of the sisters, she shall first seek the advice of the Superioress of the Motherhouse. According to the necessity or usefulness of the expenditure, the Superioress will tell her not to carry it out without the permission of the representative of the Procurator General, who presently is Monsieur Icar.

Since this situation is the most dangerous and arduous for them, both because of the need to handle money and because of the quality of the persons involved, the sisters must see to it that, as often as possible, the Ladies of the parish come in order to be present when they serve the galley slaves. If the zeal in this charitable work cools, the Reverend Superior or even the Superioress should be informed so that help may be found from them or from their advice. Here, especially, the sisters must be more exact in the practice of their Rules, having also more time than at other places. Often, they should invoke the Holy Spirit in order to purify their thoughts, words, and actions.

For the sisters employed in hospitals

At the end of their stay at the hospital, before they leave, the sick shall again make a good confession and receive Communion.

The Sister Servant shall keep an exact account of the money and the value of the clothing of the deceased.

In the article which speaks of exhorting the sick to receive Holy Communion every Sunday, this must always be done with the consent of whoever is in charge of giving the sacraments. However, the sisters may lead the sick to ask for Holy Communion themselves. The clergy in several localities find it wrong that the sisters urge the sick to receive Communion. Often it is feared that the sick receive the sacraments just to please the sisters, and that they forego a good preparation for their reception.

The preceding article states that the sick should be given an egg or some bouillon at seven o'clock. This is too late. The sister on night duty gives food to her sickest patients at four o'clock. She must then inform the sister replacing her of this.

It seems that there is an article which prohibits or does not permit the sisters to send word of their trials and spiritual state to the Superioress of the Motherhouse. I believe this could be detrimental to some of them.

The reading of the Rules at table is not such a good thing since all the sisters are not present. It seems that it would be better to have them read after supper, when all the sisters have returned, or after dinner instead of other readings before the hour of silence.

A sister who cannot observe the Order of Day as prescribed by Rule because of her work with the sick should unite herself to it in spirit from time to time.

There must always be an Assistant when the number of sisters exceeds three. Ask the Superior General for one or notify the Superioress so that she may make an earnest request for one.

Would it not be necessary to give more of an explanation in the article which speaks of the "Blessings of the Sick" so as to indicate that the Sister Servant should request the priest who is there at the time, whether he comes from the Motherhouse or from elsewhere, to say this prayer.

A.90   (Observations on the Rules)[27]
Sisters employed in the villages

The sisters shall be careful to purge patients and to let their blood only when necessary because of the dangers associated with these procedures. As soon as the sisters are called to see the sick, they shall greet them warmly and approach them cheerfully and with good will. The sisters shall then find out how long they have been ill and shall begin administering remedies by means of cold sponges or bloodletting when the sick are adverse to the sponges. If their fever continues, the sisters shall repeat the treatments three or four times. When the fever persists, they shall let blood from the patient's foot, then begin once again to let blood from the arm until the fever goes down. When the patients have an intermittent fever with recurring shivering they shall be purged by a laxative tea. The sisters shall be very careful not to administer any remedies while a patient is shivering or sweating. Only a glass of mildly fortified water with a very small amount of theriac may be given to them just before shivering starts.

The sisters cannot observe the order of the Schoolmistresses of Paris, except in the case of the little girls. For that reason, they must receive, at any time, any girl of any age who would like to come to learn. They must have the discretion to have those girls who are timid and bashful enter a special area, welcoming them warmly even when they come at mealtime or very late. They should urge them to develop the habit of kneeling each morning and evening for prayer.

In places where there is little work to be done, the sisters must be very exact in the observance of their Rule, and must use their time well. If they have no work with which to earn part of their living, they should at least busy themselves with spinning so that linen can be made.

The sisters of the villages are far from the Motherhouse and, consequently, are far from advice on their conduct and from the help they need in surmounting their faults and small interior trials. They may always write to their Superiors on these matters; however they shall help one another by great forbearance and cordiality which gives them the freedom to communicate with one another, except in matters which would be prejudicial to another sister.

Living in the villages, it is easy to turn away from good practices and resolutions. Thus, it is necessary for the sisters to be on guard, particularly to avoid falling into the idle gossip, slander, and complaints that are common with the village people. They must especially refrain from speaking of anything that goes on among them, recalling that they are in this place by the order of Divine Providence so as to provide edification for the villagers. To cause scandal or disedification would attract chastisement on themselves and on the Company.

If the sisters are obliged to be away from their house for a long time in the service of their neighbor, they shall take a few provisions with them in case they have need of food. In this way they will not have to obtain it elsewhere. If through forgetfulness or unforeseen circumstances it becomes necessary to obtain something from the poor, the sisters shall pay them so that they do not become a burden for them. In doing this, they shall be careful to demonstrate their need so as not to be accused of satisfying a fancy.

When the sisters find themselves in an area in which the churches are dirty or neglected and where the lamps are allowed to go out, they shall notify the Superioress and ask her whether or not they should assume responsibility for taking care of them.

On instruction in school

In the article which speaks of verifying once a month the names of those who miss coming to school so that they may be reprimanded, add that some sort of reward should be given to those who are diligent in attending.

87

The Sister Servant of the hospitals

She shall respect her Assistant and shall follow her advice as often as possible in doubtful situations, so long as it does not breach the confidence of others.

She shall not reprimand another sister while either one of them is in an emotional state. In this way the sister will profit from the admonition and will not be caused to feel shame.

She shall not look for faults in the sisters. When she is notified of some fault, she shall thank the sister who informed her and shall pardon, as much as possible, the sister at fault, not showing herself to have a bad opinion of this sister.

The sister who receives the sick

She shall give notification of all money found on new arrivals and shall record it so that she can give an account of it at the necessary time.

She shall notify the doctor of the new arrivals.

The sister who serves the infirm

She shall notify the Sister Servant of those who do not eat enough, either through aversion or for other reasons, and ask her to provide what is necessary.

The sister who prepares meals on days of abstinence

If it is a locality where porridge is not eaten, the sister shall not introduce it since it is not proper food for the sick. Instead, she shall prepare some poached eggs and good buttered toast, throwing a bit of water on top of the toast before putting it in the butter.

The sister in charge of dishes

If she finds any cracked dishes, she shall be careful to put them aside and to notify the Sister Servant of the need for new ones.

The sister on night duty

As she goes on duty she shall find out from the Sister Servant if there are any sick who are in need of receiving the sacraments. Thinking that this time of darkness is that of the Devil, they should make rounds of the rooms together so that they will not be taken unawares. Thus, the sister must be on her guard and should be wary of everything in order to have recourse to God and to her guardian angel.

Since she who replaces the sister on night duty is alone in the rooms for three hours of darkness in the winter, she too shall be wary of all things.

The sister laundress

Concerning the last article on the young sisters who must do the washing, do not exclude the other sisters when the Sister Servant orders it.

The Sister laundress must have care in her placement of the linen, setting aside that which must be mended and that which no longer can be used. Likewise, she shall separate linen used by men from linen used by women.

The sister in charge of the clothes of the deceased

To the article which states that she shall buy the small necessities should be added: "by order of the Sister Servant."

It should also be added to ask for the advice of the priests for the sale of the good clothing.

A.88   Hospitals[28]

In the name of God, the Daughters of Charity shall rise precisely at four o'clock. They shall make their beds after having made their act of adoration and after having dressed. At a quarter to five, they shall begin meditation. They shall conclude it at five-thirty, and then they shall recite the Litany of Jesus and two decades of their rosary.

They all shall come to the hospital at six o'clock. They then shall empty the night vessels and basins and make the beds of the sick. Before going to the hospital, they shall each have taken a piece of bread and some wine, except on days when they receive Holy Communion. On these days, they shall content themselves with the scent of vinegar, putting some vinegar on their hands. This shall only be necessary until they become accustomed to the air in the rooms of the sick.

At seven o'clock the sisters shall have the sickest patients take a bouillon or a fresh egg for breakfast. The less sick shall take some fresh butter or cooked apples.

The Daughters of Charity shall hear Mass every day. Beforehand, however, it is necessary to have the ordered medicines given to the sick. Also, there must be great care to give bouillons at the precise times.

The Daughters of Charity who have need of breakfast shall go immediately and then return to the sick in order to console those who are close to death. They shall provide for those sick in need of instruction concerning salvation, so that they can make a general confession of their entire life. This should dispose the sick to go to confession and to receive Communion every Sunday, as long as their illness persists. It should also prepare them to receive Extreme Unction at the proper time. Those sick who will recover should be moved nevermore to offend God. If they should fail in this, they should be prepared to go to confession as soon as possible.

The Daughters shall see that the sick take dinner precisely at ten o'clock. If they are in charge of the food for the sick, they shall provide at least some veal and mutton, with a bit of beef. In the evening, some roasted and boiled meat shall be provided. At least four bouillons and three fresh eggs per day shall be given to the sick who do not eat meat.

After having cleared the table of the dinner of the poor, a Daughter shall remain at the hospital. The others shall dine precisely at eleven o'clock after having made their particular examen. During dinner, each shall take her turn reading. After Grace has been said, they shall recite a decade of their rosary. Immediately afterward, two of them shall return to the hospital. Their recreation shall be in recreating with the sick. The Daughter who had remained at the hospital shall go to the second table with the reader. After having said Grace as the others did, and after having cleared the table, these two shall go to the hospital for recreation with the sick. The other two shall go to their quarters and work at whatever needs to be done, doing as much for the linens of the poor as for their little Community.

If there is no Company of Ladies which brings the afternoon collation, the Daughters shall all come to the hospital at precisely two o'clock in order to give the sick poor a few small sweets such as toast and cooked pears.

Those who have work to do shall go to their duties, or if there is nothing urgent to be done, they shall go to the bedsides of the sick and shall try to move the new arrivals to make a general confession, instructing them beforehand on the manner in which they are to confess their sins.

At four o'clock, they shall wash the sick. They shall change soiled bedsheets, empty the vessels, and put the beds of the sick back into some order without the sick getting out of bed.

At five o'clock, they shall serve supper to the sick. After supper, the same sister will remain in the hospital that did so at dinnertime. The others shall go to supper after the particular examen which should take a good quarter of an hour. This examen shall be in the form of repetition of meditation, unless they make a half hour of meditation followed by the particular examen at a later time. There shall be reading during supper.

After Grace, which shall be at about six-thirty, the sisters shall go to the hospital. The sister who had remained at the hospital shall go to supper with the reader. Those sisters who have just returned to the hospital shall make sure that the sick are all in bed at seven o'clock, and that there is water, some wine, and a few little sweets for those who need them. At seven-thirty, all the Daughters shall come to the hospital to make their general examen aloud in the midst of the poor. They shall recite the Litany of the Blessed Virgin and shall give holy water to all the sick.

At eight o'clock, they shall go to prepare the necessities for the next day's service of the sick. They shall finish their rosary, make an act of adoration, and then go to bed at precisely nine o'clock. One sister shall stay on night duty and shall see to it that none of the sick die without having received the Last Sacraments. Until the sick first awaken, she shall recite her rosary and shall read the subject of her meditation.

The sister on night duty shall have a book to read, so long as it does not interfere with her service of the sick. After having made her meditation at three-thirty, she shall go awaken the other sisters at four o'clock. If she wishes, she may take breakfast and then go to bed, rising at nine o'clock in order to hear Mass. Another sister shall take her place in the hospital, and she shall make her meditation in the same manner as the others.

All the sisters shall take their turn staying awake at night to watch over the sick.

The Daughters shall not go out into the city and shall conduct themselves with great modesty in the Motherhouse. They shall often recall the presence of God and shall speak modestly and gently with externs. They shall act in the same way among themselves and with the sick.

I think that something should be said concerning the sisters' associating with the religious.

It is hoped that the sisters shall have at their disposal some preserves, some fruit, some sugar, and some wine so that the sick are not left with something sour if they desire some nourishment outside of mealtime.

The sisters shall take proper care of the linen of the sick.

In the hospital, there should be several holy water fonts and at least two oratories in the form of small altars.

The sisters shall have four Crucifixes to leave with the sick who have received Extreme Unction. A plenary indulgence is applied to these Crucifixes through the ejaculatory prayer, "Jesus, Mary."

They shall have four pieces of coarse cloth to put on the beds of the sick for extraordinary confessions of persons who are not from the Motherhouse.

At the hospital, there should be some small copper tubs in order to facilitate the emptying of basins. There should be two larger tubs, always filled with water, attached to the wall. These should empty into ditches or elsewhere and be used to wash the basins and vessels.

In the hospital, there should be two censers which may be lit when needed. In these should burn only sweet fragrances, such as juniper or bay seed. Sometimes old bread crusts may be burned in the furnaces. Red hot gridirons should be quenched with vinegar.

It is hoped that the girls destined to join our Company would have their beds in the hospital in order to accompany the sister on night duty.

The Daughters must care for the table napkins, spoons, cups, and plates used in serving the sick their meals. The order that the sisters must retain some for their service is not noted here.

I am not speaking of the act of adoration which, it seems to me, should be made with the poor each morning. Likewise, I am not speaking of the Benedicite and the Grace of the sick, for I do not wish to know what the men religious do. And then it seems to me that there are so many things to say in order to inspire the sisters in their actions that I should speak of these topics from time to time.

If I remember other things, I shall write them, if it pleases God.

A.40   Note on Brother Antoine

The first thing that I learned from good Brother Antoine is that we must always be united to God and totally dependent upon Him. We must attribute the glory of all things to Him and be satisfied with whatever happens. We must will only what He wills for us and be faithful to all the occasions that arise for the practice of virtue.

When I was near death, I was sorry and regretted that I would die without having served my neighbor. Henceforth, I shall dedicate the rest of my life more completely to this.

Neither the habit nor the circumstances of life make us love God. Rather it is the preparation of a heart disposed to accept His good pleasure.

I must only consider my son as a child of God and love him as such. I must bear with the privation of not seeing him for the love of God.

A.84 Manner in which They are to Treat the Sick of the Hôtel-Dieu of Saint-Denis

(1645)

The sisters shall have great care that the infirm who can eat neither bread nor meat are given bouillons and eggs alternately every three hours. They should also be given some sweets according to their needs and tastes, provided it is not detrimental to their health.

The sisters shall see to it that the very sick are washed. Through fear of canker sores, the mouths of the sick should be cleansed frequently. The sisters must also watch for gangrene.

In times of great necessity, when the very sick are unable to take bouillon or eggs, they shall be given jelly and consommé. In this case, it shall be necessary to give them small amounts frequently. The sick who do not drink wine shall have some tea or some sweetened water.

Wine is to be served to the sick only at mealtime, and the sisters shall be sure to dilute it with water.

The sick shall be given bread as long as they can eat it without harm. This bread shall be baked for two days.

For each sick person there shall be a half pound of meat put in the pot each day. From this will be made the bouillons for the day. In the evening, there shall be about a pound of roasted meat for every three sick persons. An egg shall be given with the bouillon to those who cannot eat meat.

The sick shall have breakfast at seven o'clock, dinner at ten o'clock, collation at three o'clock, and supper at five-thirty.

The sick shall eat only veal and mutton, but in the same pot shall cook the beef for the attending sisters, a quarter pound for each one. This will produce a better bouillon.

On days of abstinence, herbal bouillons shall be prepared in the morning. There shall be one egg added for every two bouillons. In summer, there shall be no eggs added to the dinner bouillon. However, in winter they may be added because herbs are not so easily procured at this time.

The sisters shall have care to make preserves and syrups at the proper seasons.

Draft of the order which the Daughters of Charity must follow at the hospital of the city of Saint-Denis in France

So as to establish this order effectively, the Elder of Saint-Denis shall be asked[29] that admissions be limited to only the very sick. Also, as a protection for the sisters,[30] it shall be determined if it is necessary for those presenting themselves for admission to have been visited by the surgeon who is paid for his work with the sick, even if he does not remain at this particular hospital.

The exercises of the sisters shall be performed[31] in much the same way as they are at the hospital at Angers. The needs of the sick shall always take precedence.

Each sister shall take her turn at providing for the nighttime needs of the sick. Although she does not stay awake all night, she shall rise two hours later than the others.

The sisters shall take turns staying awake at night when the needs of the sick require it. The sister on night duty shall awaken the others at four o'clock. She shall then go to bed and rise at nine o'clock.

The Sister Servant shall welcome the sick, wash their feet, change their shirt, and comb their hair if necessary. She shall take care to lock away any clothes and money that the poor bring with them. All items shall be noted in a register so that the belongings may be returned if a person recovers or the clothes sold if a person dies. A receipt should be kept.

According to her orders, the Sister Servant shall have the care of all the necessary provisions for the house. She may have to go to procure these provisions herself, or she may send another sister, using her time well so that neither the sick nor the sisters are inconvenienced in the service of the hospital.

The Sister Servant shall welcome persons from the outside, greeting them pleasantly, permitting them to serve the poor during the day, and making sure that time is not lost in useless conversation with them.

The Sister Servant shall try herself or get others to try to move all those sick who have not made a general confession to do so as soon as possible. Those who have made one shall be urged to make a confession covering the time since they last received the Sacrament. Caution should be taken that too much pressure on the sick be avoided. The sick shall also be urged in general to make the acts of faith, hope, and charity necessary for salvation. They shall be taught to have sorrow for all the sins of their life, and to ask for God's forgiveness with all their heart. They shall be advised to make a personal confession, revealing to their confessor all the sins which they can remember. Fear should be instilled in those who have need of it and confidence in those who are too fearful.

Whereas many of the sick will have received the sacraments during their stay in the hospital, the Sister Servant must see to it that they go to confession and receive Communion in the chapel once more in the event that they recover, advising them of those things they will have to do in order to live as good Christians. However, she shall have those sick who certainly will die make frequent confessions, preparing them to die well, helping them to detach themselves from the earth and from creatures, and instilling in them the desire for paradise. She shall do this while preserving in them sentiments of repentance and of hope in the death of Jesus Crucified, having great care that they receive the Last Sacraments after having prepared them for this.

It is the responsibility of the Sister Servant to release the sick from the hospital. In this matter, as in all others, she shall act with great gentleness and charity, as well as with good judgment and justice. She must be certain that they have been well purged and have sufficiently regained their strength. If she does not take this precaution, they may suffer a relapse. This could prove detrimental to the sick and would put too much of a burden on the Motherhouse. As soon as Our Lord had cured a sick person, He would send him on his way. Likewise the Sister Servant must send those who are cured on their way, especially the idlers and the lazy. These people are often retained too long through a natural reluctance on the part of the Sister Servant to turn them out.

If there are any sick girls at the hospital the Sister Servant shall try to place them in someone's service or she shall recommend them to some of the Ladies of the city. However, the Sister Servant shall not leave the hospital in this endeavor. The only recommendation that the Sister Servant should give is for the service owed to the sick poor. Neither she nor the other sisters shall go to take messages to the city. If it is an urgent matter, then the sisters shall have the messages taken by someone else, as always, on the advice of the Sister Servant.

The Sister Servant shall seek advice from her sisters, particularly from the sister in charge of the pharmacy since she has a better knowledge of the state of the sick. It is necessary for the Sister Servant to make this act of submission with cordiality, gentleness, and true humility, occasionally forgoing her personal judgement, except in matters of importance. Likewise, it is necessary that the sister do the same, always acquiescing to the opinions of the Sister Servant when she sees no notable interest in her opinions either for the glory of God or for the service of her neighbor.

All the sisters shall always strive for true union, being on guard to avoid appearances to the contrary when habits, naturally bad dispositions, and bad moods contribute to opposing frames of mind. They shall always remember to honor the union of the Blessed Trinity, by which all order in the world has been made and is conserved, and to which, as they should recall, they submit themselves.

The Sister Pharmacist shall have great care to keep the drugs in a good state, making sure that nothing spoils nor is lost. She shall see to it that all her utensils are kept clean, that the sick are given their medications at the necessary times, and that the doctor and surgeon are asked to come when necessary. She shall be particularly obliged to inform the Sister Servant of the state of the sick so that, by her order, the sacraments may be given to them. Likewise, she shall only carry out her responsibilities on the orders of the Sister Servant.

The Sister Pharmacist or another of the sisters shall let the blood of the sick and dress their wounds when it becomes necessary and the surgeon is not present. Also, the Sister Pharmacist shall be informed that her position shall not hinder her from performing other duties at the Motherhouse. For instance, when the Sister Servant is not present, or when the Sister Servant orders it, she shall receive the sick as the Sister

Servant herself would. She shall wash the dishes, do the laundry, and take her turn at night duty, except when she is kept busy by her own duties and the Sister Servant feels it appropriate to excuse her from these duties. Then the Sister Servant herself shall carry out these duties in her turn. She must be the first one to give to the others the example of virtue and of work.

The Sister Portress shall be very exact in her duties. She shall let no one enter the house without the permission of the Sister Servant, and she shall serve the sick in her turn as do the other sisters, always carrying out her own duties, except on days when she has night duty. In this case, one of the other sisters shall carry out her duties the following morning.

The Sister Servants shall determine who must keep[32] the register of the admission and release — by death or otherwise — of the sick. There shall be three registers. In the register of admission shall be noted the year, month, and day of the entrance of the sick; their name; their status; and from where they come. An identification ticket shall be put on the arms of the sick, and one shall also be put with their clothes in safekeeping. The sisters shall be most careful to save any letters or important papers that they find in the clothing. They must also be sure to notify the relatives of those who die. In case of recovery, the relatives should be notified of any necessities.

In the second register shall be noted the names of the sick who recover and the duration of their stay in the hospital.

In the third register shall be noted the names of the dead and the localities from which they came. The length of their illnesses shall also be noted, along with any business which they have entrusted to the sisters. With counsel, all such business must be carried out as soon as possible.

The Sister Servant and all the other sisters shall have great care in the management of the house so that the well-being of the poor shall be preserved there. They shall try their best to increase this well-being through the knowledge that persons on the outside have of the sisters' good order, and especially through the knowledge of the sisters' careful service of the poor and of the edification that they give. This good example must be given as much to those who visit the hospital as to the sick themselves, who will always be witnesses to the charitable conduct of the sisters.

The sisters shall allow none of their acquaintances to eat or sleep at the aforementioned hospital, even their Sisters of Charity, unless they bring the necessary provisions as they have been ordered and unless they have permission to go there.

Apart from the above, the sisters shall adapt, as far as possible, to the order of day and the practices observed at the House of the Directress who resides in Paris. In light of this, they shall have a copy of these practices which they shall read from time to time along with the above.

A.91b   Rule for the Motherhouse

The elected officers:
  The Superioress
  The First Assistant
  The Treasurer
  The Procuratrix
  The Directress of
    the Seminary

The appointed officers:
  The Bell-Ringer
  The Schoolmistress
  The Portress
  The Pharmacist
  The Baker
  The Cook
  The Gardener
  The Laundress

Obligations of the Superioress

After her election, having given herself totally to God for the accomplishment of His most holy will in this very important matter, she must desire to be entirely detached from any concern for herself.

1. Her principal care is to see to it that the Rule is exactly observed. She does this by *gentle persuasion* rather than through constraint. She must instill it in the minds of her sisters first by her example and then by her words.

2. She must believe herself most incapable of solid virtue since God has chosen her to serve the others. In this way, the shame of not meeting the standards which she sets for others will help her to acquire self-knowledge.

She shall consider herself the beast of burden of the Company, loaded with a precious treasure of which she must give a most exact account. When there is a general or particular question concerning the welfare of the Company, she shall not take herself into consideration. In this matter, she shall always do more to advance the spiritual welfare of the Company. Nevertheless, she must have great care for its temporal welfare, exhibiting great confidence in Divine Providence in both endeavors.

3. Since she cannot undertake such a heavy task alone, she shall rely on her Sister Officers, but without shifting responsibility for everything as if she were alone. She shall never appear to be inconvenienced when her counsel or permission is sought. She shall watch continuously over all that happens in the Company, whether it be in the House, or in the parishes and countryside. In order to sadden no one, she must keep this watch without causing uneasiness and without letting it be known how she is aware of what happens.

4. She shall watch over herself so that her heavy workload does not cause her stress. This makes it difficult for the sisters to approach her and difficult for her to speak cordially with them.

5. She shall do her utmost to prevent the sisters from knowing her weakness; not letting herself get carried away in speaking with one sister of another; and not acting on her first impulses but having enough discretion to discern the proper times to advise them of their shortcomings.

She must try to be easy to approach, so that her sisters may speak to her with confidence, but she must also be discreet so as to give them no reason to lose respect for her.

In order to attract the sisters to perfection, the Superioress should instill in them a sense of esteem for the Rule rather than fear of chastisement in the event that they are unfaithful.

She shall confer often with her Sister Officers in general, and sometimes with them individually. In this way, she gains knowledge of what is taking place in the Company, and she is able to notify her Officers of needs or make comments on things which have been brought to her attention. This she must do with great cordiality and gentleness, considering her Officers as part of herself.

She shall try not to sadden the sisters in the practice of their Rule, having as much forbearance as possible when one of her orders has not been carried out, accepting it so long as it is not something of notable detriment to the Company.

She shall instill esteem for the Sister Officers in the other sisters so that they may put the Officers' advice to good use without ever sensing her disapproval of their conduct unless there is a strong reason why they should.

She shall add nothing nor take away anything from the practice of the Rule. However, she may dispense the sisters from some practices according to their needs, but not permanently without having received an order from the Superior, as is the case in everything of any importance.

She shall be extremely careful never to say anything nor write anything in behalf of the Superior without his knowledge and approval for fear of inappropriately involving him in some matter. Insofar as she is able, she shall carry the keys to the entrance of the House. When she is unable to do so, the first Assistant shall take on this responsibility.

The Superioress shall be exact in responding to the letters of the sisters away from the House. She shall use this opportunity to assist them in their struggle for perfection, showing her esteem for their virtue and good will, and only showing knowledge of their faults when it is of great necessity.

She must be careful not to repeat anything told to her in secret regarding another sister for fear that it will take away the sisters' confidence in her. In advising the sisters of their faults, she must use great prudence, never doing it immediately, if this can be avoided, nor unnecessarily, but advising them, nevertheless, carefully, gently, and cordially.

Office of the First Assistant

Words of excuse shall be few and words of refusal even fewer as the First Assistant and the other officers acquiesce in the election. The First Assistant must humble herself, along with the others, having fear of not being able to carry out her obligations properly, but also having confidence that God will give her the ability to do that which she could not do on her own. She shall fix in her mind the belief that she must carry out her duties with submission to her Superioress, doing nothing without first informing her and refraining from ordering anything that she would not allow. Moreover, she should hide nothing from her, however disagreeable, that had occurred in the Company. She should believe and act in such a way that the other sisters will perceive that she has no power to act or to give orders except in keeping with the directives which she herself has received or in the absence of the Superioress.

If she is unable to give advice when the sisters request it of her in matters of any importance, she shall not send them to the Superioress but shall tell them that she will speak to the Superioress on the matter.

Since she has the same obligation as the Superioress to see to the observance of the Rule, she shall watch over everything in order to advise her Sister Officers of any shortcomings in their exercises, doing so gently and charitably and likewise accepting advice given her. If obedience causes her to be absent, she shall notify the Second Assistant so that nothing is omitted which must be done. She shall try in everything she does to set a good example for the whole Community through the modesty, exactitude, and charity which mark her recollection as a result of God's presence.

She shall not weary of advising her sisters of their faults or of what they should be doing, keeping in mind that repeated acts are necessary in order to destroy a habit and to establish another one in its place. She shall not act as those who would rather find fault immediately with the sisters than talk with them about the practice of virtue repeatedly over a period of time. Such persons do not consider their obligation or the good which can result from instilling the idea of virtue and work in others.

Her principal care shall be to see the sisters who

are not following the Rule well. In so doing, she shall learn the details of the situation and shall advise them of their faults. All this shall be presented in her report to the Superioress. This report shall be given with simplicity, an open heart, and great charity every week, if possible, or when the Superioress orders it.

The Office of the Treasurer

Besides taking the place of the Superioress in the absence of both the Superioress and the First Assistant, the Treasurer shall see to it that the Rule is observed and that each sister has a task. She shall have a key to the safe and one to the collection box in which the daily receipts are kept. In the presence of the Superioress, she shall give one hundred francs to the Procuratrix monthly and then enter the sum in the register. As far as possible, she shall also receive the monthly report of the Procuratrix in the presence of the Superioress. If the Treasurer notices any extraordinary or excessive expenditure, she shall make the matter clear and then gently and charitably inform the Superioress, since she cannot remedy the situation on her own. If the Superioress does not notice that three hundred pounds are being kept in the collection box, then the Treasurer shall humbly advise her to put the money in the safe.

She shall do her utmost to see to it that the money is managed well so that no debts arise. She shall draw up her reports in good time so that they may be given annually, without fail, before the Superior or whomever the Charity dictates.

Office of the Procuratrix

The Sister Procuratrix shall write down exactly the daily expenditures, receiving an exact account from the sisters who purchase the daily provisions, making sure that the normal expenditure is not surpassed. She shall introduce no changes in the management of the household, and she shall make sure that nothing is wasted. If a wasteful situation arises, one for which she has no solution, then she shall notify the Superioress of it as soon as possible in order to prevent it in the future.

She shall see to it that the provisions are bought at the proper time. For this reason, she shall advise the Superioress to ascertain whether or not there is money at the House. To insure good management, she shall retain the key to the pantry so as to keep an eye on the kitchen sister and to see to it that nothing spoils. This is necessary so that the little that the sisters receive may be well prepared and for the general well-being of the household.

Office of the Directress of the Seminary

The Sister Directress of the Seminary shall have particular care in considering the duties of her office and in acquiring the virtues necessary to perform them well. She shall rid herself of her passions in order to act without personal interest and, if possible, without following her own judgment. However, she should often implore the help of the Holy Spirit so that she may see her sisters and their actions only in His light. Whether these sisters are at the House or in the parishes, the Sister Directress shall give a truthful account of anything she notices in them whenever she is sent to them or they to her. That which is certain shall be reported as such and doubtful matters as doubtful. When the sisters from the parishes come to the House for confession, she shall make sure that the entrance of the confessional is guarded, for fear of noise. If the entrance is not locked, she shall station a sister there.

From time to time, she shall go through the House in order to discourage frivolity and the frequent gossiping, murmuring, and news telling that occurs among the sisters coming in and the sisters at the House. Such activity is contrary to good preparation for confession.

In carrying out this duty, she must use great prudence and gentleness, advising the sisters of what they have to do and pleasantly enduring the arguments of those who are most attached to these conversations. She shall make them understand that it is her duty which requires her to take such a stand and that they will not think bad of it once they become accustomed to it.

From time to time she shall most truthfully and charitably give an account of her office to the Superioress.

The principal concern of this Sister shall be to watch over the new sisters, studying their moods and aptitudes for the first week or two.

She shall confer with the Superioress on this matter so that together they can determine the proper placement and training of the sisters.

These first two weeks — or longer — she shall instruct the new sisters to say their rosary at the time when the community begins meditation. Through prayers to the Blessed Virgin and St. Joseph, they shall ask God to give them the grace to make meditation whenever obedience to the Rule permits them to do so.

At six o'clock, she shall leave the chapel with the new sisters in order to instruct them in their faith, their Christian obligations, and in all that is necessary for their salvation.

When new sisters arrive who have already received sufficient instruction, the Directress shall point out to them the necessity that the Sisters of Charity have of recalling their first formation. She shall also stress that they should have no desire to change food or clothing except in order to imitate more closely the way of life of their Masters, the poor, for whom they must always have respect.

She must advise the new sisters of their faults against modesty, teaching them the way in which they are accountable for their actions in this matter. She shall teach them the proper behavior with regard to the older sisters, advising them to ask forgiveness of these older sisters as soon as they realize that they have failed in their duty. She shall also teach them the proper behavior with regard to the other new sisters.

During the second month, she shall teach them how to make mental prayer, instructing them in the practice of one point each day. Simply and succinctly she shall explain one article of the Rule each day, advising them that failure in some of them puts them in danger of committing a mortal sin against the commandments of God.

At two o'clock, after the Community reading, the Seminary Directress shall go with the new sisters to their designated place and shall instruct them in the excellence of the Sacraments, teaching the sisters that it is through the merit of the Blood of Jesus Christ that the benefits of the sacraments are bestowed upon us. She shall inform them of the great happiness experienced by souls who receive the sacraments well, and of the unhappiness of those who do not. She shall have them give an account of their use of the morning with regard to faults against their Rule and against the sisters. She shall teach them the acts necessary to prepare for a good confession and Communion, although this would only be for a week. Esteem due the confessors must also be taught at this time.

I omitted that, at one o'clock, she shall have them say the "Our Father", or another prayer for those who do not know it. This shall continue until the two o'clock bell.

When the Superioress or another of the Sister Officers employs one of the new sisters, they shall make sure that it is not during her instruction time; and the sister who has been given a task shall notify the Seminary Directress. The Directress shall never indicate disapproval; however, if she finds the situation inconvenient, she shall go to consult with the Superioress on the matter and then shall gently inform the sister making the request.

Office of the Bell-Ringer

The sister who awakens the others must pay attention to her responsibility, which is comparable to that of our guardian angels. Each evening, she shall ask her own guardian angel for help so that she will have bell in hand precisely at four o'clock. For the sake of health and modesty, she will have decently dressed beforehand.

She shall go quietly to all parts of the dormitories, saying in a moderately loud voice, "In the name of God arise, my Sisters."

At four-thirty she shall ring the call to chapel.

At five-fifteen, the Angelus.

At eleven-thirty, dinner.

At twelve-fifteen, the rising from table is rung and the reader says Grace. The sister who serves at table is usually one of the Sister Officers.

At six o'clock, the suppertime examen, and at eight o'clock, evening prayers.

Office of the Portress

The Sister Portress shall often think of the trust that the others have in her in giving her such an important duty. As do the other Officers, she shall ask for the grace to perform her duties well. Since she is by herself, she shall be sure to have some work which she can carry with her so that time is not wasted.

She shall not converse on curious or worldly matters with those waiting at the entrance. Often, these are poor people, and she shall do her utmost to give them some manner of advice. She shall do the same for the novices.

She shall not go far from the door, so that those who come are not kept waiting; and she shall humbly ask forgiveness of anyone who complains of having waited too long.

When someone rings to enter or exit, the sound warns her to speak and conduct herself with modesty. When a sister is asked for, and the Portress does not know whether she is present, she shall ask the person to be seated while she goes to notify the Superioress or, in her absence, the Sister Assistant. The response shall be relayed simply to the person waiting, and the sister asked for shall not be told that she has had a visitor.

Likewise, the Portress shall give no messages to the sisters nor tell them that someone wished to speak with them. However, if someone begs them to do so, then she shall faithfully tell the Superioress.

She must be careful of things told her in general conversation with externs so that confusion does not arise from her lack of knowledge of news from the city.

She shall have great care always to carry with her the keys to the door, never leaving them there. She shall close the other doors of the courtyard entrance and shall let no one enter without permission.

She shall have the sick wait to be bled or bandaged in the St. Cosmas Room. The school girls shall be placed in the school and the novices in the nearby parlor. She shall ask the wealthy and moderately wealthy to sit in the St. Peter parlor, keeping the door to the refectory closed.

Before nightfall in winter, she shall be sure to double lock the door, and she shall be sure never to go there alone. She shall not open the door without permission after seven-thirty in winter and eight o'clock in summer. At nine o'clock, after having locked all doors of access, she shall take her keys to the Superioress. If there was some trouble in locking any of the doors, she shall notify the Superioress of it.

Office of the Schoolmistress

The Schoolmistress shall have her sister students read from six o'clock until seven when they must go to Mass except those who put the dormitories in order and the sister who is responsible for the community room and the downstairs area. They shall make their meditation by themselves in the chapel after the lessons given by the First Assistant or, in case of necessity, by another appointed for this task.

At precisely eight o'clock, she shall go to the school and kneel down to ask for help of the Holy Spirit for herself and for her pupils, that they be taught purely for the glory of God.

She shall make sure that all the pupils coming to school do the same thing.

She shall have her little girls recite their lessons attentively, not merely going through the motions. She shall often reflect that these souls must learn from her the means to attain their salvation. God asks this of her; the children's parents give her this responsibility; and the interest of these poor children urges her to it. At ten-thirty, she shall take her pupils to Mass, placing them all in front of her in order to get them used to behaving respectfully and appropriately in church. On their return, she shall have them enter the House, praising those who have done well, and gently reprimanding those who have not, emphasizing to them the importance of this matter. She shall advise them to return home with modesty, to respect and obey their parents, and to avoid offending God. She then shall get them all together as soon as possible so that they can go to the dinnertime examen.

At one o'clock in the afternoon, she shall go to the appointed place in order to instruct those sisters who have permission to learn to write. Carefully, and without noise, each one shall write only four lines. Those who finish first shall be sent back to the House. Those who have difficulty learning their prayers by heart shall be asked to recite them after the writing lessons are finished. Following the instruction, which takes place after the two o'clock reading, she shall go to the school, entering as she had in the morning. Provided that it is done slowly and attentively when there are a great many pupils, she shall have them recite their lessons, although not so much as they had done in the morning. Especially in the winter, the Schoolmistress shall ask for help from the Superioress so that nothing is omitted.

She shall not fail to have her pupils pray to God every morning and every evening before she sends them home.

She shall place greater importance on instructing them well in the mysteries of faith, in correct morality, and on the difference between good and evil than on progress in reading or on the memorization of a lot of facts which reveal more curiosity and vanity than solid learning which consists in understanding clearly what has been taught and putting it to good use.

She shall instruct her pupils well in the sacraments and in the esteem due to them. She shall teach them all that is necessary for the proper reception of these sacraments.

In order that the souls to which she speaks may profit from her advice, she shall inflame in herself a great love for the salvation of these souls and a great esteem for her work. She shall recognize herself unworthy of this task and shall be sure never to give them bad example, correcting them impartially, and conducting herself always with modesty.

She shall never accept anything which her pupils would like to give her, not even a New Year's gift. However, if it is something quite small and sent by a child's mother, then she shall accept it with the permission of the Superioress.

Each Thursday she shall teach Catechism, explaining it so that it is understood and phrasing her questions in different ways so that her pupils grasp the meaning rather than simply memorize words.

She shall teach them the way in which they are to spend their day, making them accountable for it. She shall take special care to instruct them when it comes time to prepare them for their First Communion; indicating to them that they will possibly receive more important graces for their salvation from it, if they are open to its reception.

Office of the Pharmacist

Her primary concern is to learn properly the method of compounding remedies; and she shall be most exact to observe all that is necessary in this. She shall only use pure drugs, checking on them often. In the event that some remedy deteriorates, she shall make some up new immediately.

She shall prepare syrups in the proper seasons. In this endeavor, she shall follow the exact proportions and shall do everything promptly, neither overcooking nor undercooking the syrups.

Since her responsibilities involve the health of the Company, she shall have greater care for the health of her soul so that all her care may be pleasing to God.

When the sisters tell her of their indispositions, she shall listen to them charitably without dispensing remedies too often. She shall then inform the Superioress of what she finds out. Without exception, she shall have equal care of all the sisters. In the case of illness, she shall carefully give whatever is needed to the sisters. She shall be discreet so that nothing she says will sadden them; she shall sympathize with those who have need of sympathy; and she shall encourage the fainthearted and apprehensive, helping them to submit themselves to the will of God.

She shall inform the Superioress of any need in the quality of their food or of any need of the sacraments. She shall also inform the Superioress when the sick have need of being visited in order to prevent great despondency.

When it becomes necessary to call a doctor, she shall make this known, and she shall be most exact to prepare the prescriptions. She shall make sure that the sister appointed as Sister Infirmarian carries out her duty well; that she gives nothing to the sick which could cause them harm; that she does not tell them anything which could sadden them, nor anything which is said at the House; that she gives nothing which is served at the sisters' meals.

Insofar as she is able, she shall be the one who bandages and bleeds the poor who come to the House. She shall find out from the Superioress which sisters may learn these skills so that they can assist her. She shall be a great example to the sisters of the House and to those outside as well since the office which she occupies is one of the principal ones. She must be careful that all she says is to the point. She must also be careful of the words she chooses; nothing she utters should cause disedification.

She shall particularly refrain from being curious and from wanting to know what goes on in the houses of the sisters. Insofar as is possible, she shall make sure that no one is bled who has the means to go to a surgeon to have it done. Others in need of being bled and Ladies who do not appear to be very sick shall not be bled unless they are well-known by the Sister Pharmacist, or, at least, not without the advice of a doctor. A pregnant woman is never bled without the advice of a doctor.

As is the custom, the Sister Pharmacist shall sell good quality remedies at a better price than is found at the apothocary shops.

She shall maintain an account book in which to record money owed her, and all entries shall be crossed out promptly when she has been paid.

She shall have a strong box in the pharmacy in which she shall place all money received, and she shall have a key to it so that she can take money from it for her advance payments. Every three months, she shall count the money along with the Superioress and the Treasurer. She shall record funds given out as the Treasurer records money taken in.

If it becomes necessary to make large advance payments for supplies, she shall borrow the money from the House and then repay it from her receipts before they are totaled.

Office of the Baker

She shall greatly esteem her duty since bread is the greatest necessity for life. She shall always try to do her best without, nonetheless, blending her flour any differently than normal.

She shall make sure that her oven is neither too hot

nor too cold, and in order to regulate this better, she shall split some wood and leave it to dry at the oven after having done her baking.

She shall be most exact and faithful that no dainties such as cakes or other pastries are baked. She shall also make sure that none of the sisters come to take away bread or to break the loaves.

She shall be careful that the flours are blended again and that the bran does not go bad. She shall keep the granary in good condition.

When kneading the dough, she shall not use water which is too hot, for this produces a coarser, red bread. The baker shall spare neither herself nor her sweat for she shall knead the dough much more than is actually necessary. Once in a while she may rest before she finishes.

The Office of the Cook

This is one of the most important offices for the regulation of the House. For this reason, the Cook shall animate herself for her task as if she were continually in a hurry. Nevertheless, she shall do this without overeagerness. In the evening, she shall be careful to have some water and wood with which to start her cooking early in the morning.

At four-thirty she shall go to the chapel as the others, and shall make her meditation in peace. After the Angelus has rung, she shall leave the chapel and go immediately to start the fire and to put on the pot which she shall not leave until it is at a full boil. Her fire having been started, she shall complete, in the kitchen, the prayers which are said at this time, checking on the fire from time to time.

After her pot has come to a boil, she shall go to Mass, unless there is an infirm individual in need of soup, in which case she shall prepare some and then leave, with permission.

If one day she finds that the herbs had not been cleaned the night before, she then shall ask a sister to help her. On other days as well, she shall ask for help rather than have dinner ready any later than exactly eleven-thirty.

When one of the Ladies or some other woman in retreat is present, she shall have extra care that their meals are ready on time.

She shall not wait until close to dinnertime and then hurry about her business. Rather, she shall work carefully all morning long, finding out well in advance what she is to prepare for the meal.

She shall keep herself clean and shall work in a clean manner so that nothing distasteful is found in the soup and portions.

She shall accept corrections and reprimands with humility and with the desire to profit from them.

She shall be sure to prepare enough so that each one receives an equal portion.

She shall see to it that the meat is neither overcooked nor undercooked. She shall season fricasseed meat well without its being too spicy, too salty, or too vinegary since all this is bad for the health. On the other hand, it should not lack seasoning to the point that the sisters cannot eat it.

She shall dish out the soup precisely at eleven-fifteen so that everyone can be served peacefully, promptly, and quietly. Otherwise, service could be interrupted.

At five o'clock, she shall start to prepare supper. If there are any infirm individuals or women in retreat, then she shall start at four-thirty and well before. She shall go to the chapel at five-thirty to listen to the reading, and there she shall have a quarter hour of meditation. She shall conclude her meditation in the kitchen for she must be ready to serve the sisters when they arrive at the refectory at a little before six-fifteen. . .

L.134   Rule for the Sisters Going to Le Mans
(Wednesday, May 2, 1646)

Sister Jeanne Lepintre shall go to Le Mans with a heart filled with charity for the sick poor, for the sisters who are accompanying her, and for those whom she will find there.

She shall take great care to bear with and to edify the first Daughters whom she will encounter at the Hôtel-Dieu. She shall try very gently to bring them back to the practice of their Rule in keeping with the orders of Monsieur Portail. She shall show them cordial respect. The sisters shall have great respect for the Administrators and obedience to the Superior of the Mission.

As often as possible the sisters shall send us news, notifying us of what is taking place among them and informing us of other necessary matters.

Even if there is a pharmacist, they shall take on the task of washing the women and girls.

They shall recall often the advice of Monsieur Vincent, especially that which prohibits unnecessary communication with men, and even clergy, in any place outside of the church or hospital.

They shall remember to preserve great gentleness and support among themselves; and it should be with an open heart and great trust that they approach the Sister Servant for all their needs.

They shall give my regards to all the Priests of the Mission and shall show them great respect. They shall not take advantage of their gentleness and goodness and shall conduct themselves towards them as they would at the House.

While en route, they shall remember to follow their Rule as precisely as they are able. After they leave the coach, they shall go to adore the Blessed Sacrament at the church. The sister sent to the inn for necessities shall conduct herself with reserve. If they have some time, they shall go to the hospital to visit any of the sick poor who might be there, recalling that the love and service of God and neighbor is their sole reason for existence.

L.131   Note on the Subjects Which Need to Be Treated During the Conferences[33]

(1646)

To help us to understand the nature of the calling of the Daughters of Charity and the dispositions that this vocation requires. To this end, to point out the esteem they must have for their state in life and for the poor since they are paid and nourished from the funds provided for them.

What the sisters are to do to avoid receiving in this world their recompense for the service they render to the poor. This could happen because of the slight effort they put into a service which they no longer perform but for which they receive great honor.

If the sisters do not sometimes deceive themselves in their overeagerness to serve the poor of the parishes or in the Hôtel-Dieu, which can cause them to be less satisfied to remain in the House.

If those sisters who remain in the House do not have the same merit as those engaged in the direct service of the poor.

What care and affection the sisters should have for the Rule of the House and how faithful they should be in observing it.

How the sisters must esteem and love one another and be willing to have their faults reported to the one who holds the place of Superioress. How each one in turn should warn the same Superioress of the faults which they have seen her commit.

How each sister should spontaneously remind her companions of their faults and how they should accept these admonitions.

On the danger to be found in complaining to one another of the faults they find in their sisters, and particularly in murmuring and in unburdening themselves to others about the admonitions they have received.

A.44 Remarks on Three Deceased Sisters

(c. 1646)

Among other reasons which we have for speaking of our deceased sisters, the little progress in virtue which is apparent among us is one of the most important.

Another is to avoid being ungrateful for the graces which we receive from the goodness of God.

The three sisters of whom we are to speak all died young. This is a third reason pushing us to have this Conference as soon as possible: so that we may all, young and old alike, place ourselves in the dispositions in which we wish to be found at the moment of death.

Our Sister Marie who died at Saint-Denis had only been in the Company for about three months. Nevertheless, she practiced almost all the virtues that could be asked of her, particularly great submission and the desire to persevere and to die in the Company. She hid her ailments and placed such little importance on her life that her physical limitations never prevented her from undertaking the most arduous chores.

Retreat note: fear of leaving the Company.

Sister Jacquette Midy had a strong desire to die in the Company. Since she was aware that she did not have sufficient physical strength to remain, she hoped to die rather than be obliged to leave. She greatly desired to do penance. She patiently accepted being admonished of her faults. Although she had considerable difficulty in overcoming her self-will, she submitted to others very peacefully. She asked pardon for not having said from what region she came.

As for our Sister Marie Despinal,[34] from the time that she sought to enter the Company, she revealed a true call from God to perseverance. She showed no imperfections.

A.75 (On the Conduct of Divine Providence)
The day and the season when God permitted us to recognize His Divine Providence by the remarkable events surrounding the fall of our ceiling[35] reminded me once again of my profound interior conversion at that time when His goodness gave me light and understanding concerning the great anxieties and difficulties which I was then experiencing.

I then thought that our entire family should have great devotion to the Feast of Pentecost and total dependence on Divine Providence. However, this should be manifested in a very particular way.

As on other occasions when the grace of God has acted in our Most Honored Father and in the souls of some of our sisters, leading to the solid foundation of this little family, so it seemed to me that rather than looking upon this event as an accident, we should see it as a warning to His Charity to establish a close union between the way of life that God wanted this community to practice and that of his Institute, since there are common interests to be found in this grace of God. Miserable as I am, I should have seen this accident as a punishment for my sins. However, I never thought of it in that light either at the time or later. In word and in my heart, I always considered that it was a grace from God, permitted for an end that we do not know and that God, by means of it, was asking something of each of us. I pray that He will reveal His will to our Most Honored Father.

It seemed to me that in order to be faithful to God we must live in great union with one another. Since the Holy Spirit is the union of the Father and the Son, the life which we have freely undertaken must be lived in this great union of hearts. This will prevent us from becoming annoyed by the actions of others and enable us to bear with one another and to live together with cordiality and gentleness. The familiar exchanges that we propose to have each Friday and the monthly Conferences, should we be permitted to have them, can help to facilitate this practice. We should also ask the extraordinary confessor for means for acquiring this virtue as well as that of total dependence on Divine Providence, since this is one of the virtues which God clearly requires of us in order to insure the preservation of the Company.

We must once again be taught by this voice of God to become accustomed, out of love, to think often of Him so as to prepare ourselves to die at the time that pleases Him and even suddenly, if such be His holy will, since our lives place us in situations where this could happen. We must often reflect upon this.

As for myself, I thought that I must be more faithful to God than ever before in my spiritual life, in the service I must render to the poor, and especially in the guidance and assistance which I bring to our sisters. I must also ask for direction in the use I am to make of the many graces which I see God bestowing upon me and with which I feel interiorly filled.

Once, moved by this sentiment, I thought that I ought to refuse these graces and desire only God. However, a few days later, God led me to understand that the graces which He granted to me were not for me, but because I belonged to Him as I was. Nevertheless, I did not understand this.

With all my heart, I wanted to render glory to God and to cause others to do the same, since this seemed to correspond to the plan of God when He permitted this accident to happen to us. To this end, I thought that I must strive to keep the memory of this event alive within me for the rest of my days and thank God for the interior sentiments which He gave me at that time.

I resolved to ask permission for myself and for all of our sisters to receive Holy Communion each month on this date, so as to thank God for His protection and for the grace which He has given to us in calling us to serve Him in the person of the poor and to renew the fervor of the first days of our vocation to the Company.

Each year, from the Ascension to Pentecost, all our sisters shall practice interior recollection in honor of the plan of the Son of God when He commanded His Apostles to remain in a state of inactivity while awaiting the coming of the Holy Spirit. They shall strive to imitate the life of the Blessed Virgin and the Apostles in their deprivation of the visible presence of Jesus. Henceforth, if possible, the sisters of the Motherhouse shall make their retreat at this time. With permission, they shall be deprived of Holy Communion so as to do penance for their failings in the reception of the Blessed Sacrament during the course of the year and to obtain from God better dispositions for the future.

Let us all make a pilgrimage to invoke the intercession of the saints and to glorify God for the graces which He has bestowed on the entire Company on this occasion. On this date each month, the sisters shall say the Litany of the Saints at the conclusion of the evening meditation.

A.49b Prayer to Be Said Morning and Evening Before the Examination of Conscience

I adore You, Most Holy Trinity, one God in three Persons, and I thank You for all the graces that, in Your goodness, You have bestowed upon me. I give you my heart and all that I possess so that henceforth I may accomplish Your holy will.

Grant me the grace, I beg of You, my God, to spend this day without offending You and without wronging my neighbor. Help me to recognize my sins and move me to contrition for having offended You, my God, who are so good. Have mercy on us because of the merits of the Precious Blood of my Savior. Have mercy on us and on all souls immersed in mortal sin so that, having obtained mercy, they may praise You eternally.

Period Between 1647 and 1660

A.85 (Instructions to the Sisters Who Were Sent to Montreuil)

(1647)

Our Sisters Anne Hardemont and Marie Lullen are going to Montreuil in order to discover what Divine Providence wishes them to do there.

First and foremost, they must remember to keep in mind God and His glory. Then they must consider the welfare of the people with whom they will be associated in order to serve them better according to their aptitudes.

Thirdly, they shall remember that none of their actions among themselves or with externs should be prejudicial to the Company of the Daughters of Charity because we must honor God in the interest of the Company.

Above all, they shall beware of crediting to themselves the least portion of the works in which God does us the honor of employing us. This can come about through vain complacency, satisfaction, or self-serving plans; all things which we must renounce often.

En route, they shall be as exact as possible in the practice of their Rule. If they cannot make their morning meditation before leaving, they shall make it without fail while in the coach. Before leaving their bedroom, they shall make an act of adoration. In the evening they shall make their examen while kneeling.

They shall take a book along with them in order to read in the coach. They shall try to keep their exercises private and shall avoid bothering others in the coach.

They shall guard against uttering improper, careless or idle words, and against any unbecoming action. In order to prevent this, they shall watch over one another in order to give a charitable warning if a sister accidentally forgets herself. The sister given the warning shall willingly accept it even if she is not aware of her fault.

If they have the opportunity to say a few good words to some poor person or to the servants at the inns, they should do so with humility, never mocking the person's ignorance.

After leaving the coach, before thinking about eating, they shall go to the nearest church to adore God in the Blessed Sacrament.

They shall make the same act of adoration in every village through which they pass. They shall acknowledge the guardian angel of each town and the guardian angels of each soul living there in order to commend them to their protection for the glory of God.

If they are able to do so before the coach departs in the afternoon, they shall visit some of the sick or the hospital, if there is one in the village.

Arriving at Montreuil, they shall go directly to the church and then to the Château to pay their respects to the Governor, the Count of Lannoy, telling him that they are there to receive his orders.

They shall remember that true Daughters of Charity must be united in order to fulfill God's expectations. Because our corrupted nature has deprived us of this perfection, and since sin separates us from our unity which is God, following the example of the Blessed Trinity, we must have but one heart and act with one mind as do the three divine Persons. We must do this in such a way that, when the sister in charge of the sick requests the help of her sister, the sister who instructs the children shall readily comply. And, if the sister in charge of the children requests assistance from the sister in charge of the poor, she shall do likewise since both tasks are equally the business of God. Considering themselves both chosen by Divine Providence in order to act in unison, we hope never to hear the words "That is your business, not mine."

If they are housed outside of the hospital, they shall not go to the hospital unless the Count orders them to do so.

If they are housed at the hospital and their only task seems to be the service of the poor of the city, and, nonetheless, the Count wishes them to take charge of the school for girls and the care of the sick of the hospital as well, then they shall comply and shall not involve themselves in other things.

Should the Count request that they tell him all that happens at the hospital, then they shall do so with great prudence and charity.

Prudence consists in speaking about important matters only and not relating a lot of trifles that are not worth saying. That which you feel obliged to say should be expressed in as gentle a manner as possible; remembering that what seems evil is often so only in our feelings and opinions. In order to avoid conflict with the women and girls who have run the hospital for a long time, our sisters must have a great respect for them and manifest great love and cordiality toward them. The sisters shall do nothing without their permission, not even take a pot, a frying pan, or anything else for their own needs.

In this matter, they shall remember the instruction and example of Our Most Honored Father: that they shall enter this house prepared to suffer and to humble themselves beyond all their expectations. This they can do by apologizing to persons apparently angry with them even if they did not provoke this anger.

If some of these good women and girls get the idea that you are there to dismiss them and send them away, in the name of God, my Sisters, bear with such little suspicions, but prevent them as much as you can from arising by showing submission and cordiality in your words and actions. Consider that, in reality, you must respect these good persons as your mothers and as persons chosen by God to begin this work and to administer it so well during all these years.

Never respond to any complaints or reproaches that they may address to you. Although you are assured that the Count will provide for all your needs, do not take advantage of this, and bear in mind that you are there on a trial basis. If these good girls do fairly well and you, on the contrary, are at odds among yourselves and exhibit discord, you shall most certainly be sent back. This fact shall oblige you to act always with purity of intention, only looking upon God with more humility, mistrusting yourselves and trusting in God so that, if we are sent back, we shall be able to believe that it is the will of God; that it will not harm the Company nor give bad example to anyone.

Consequently, you must go there with the intention of accomplishing the will of God as manifested through the will of the Count; and in order to obey the Count more perfectly, you shall consider him in God and God in him. Remember that such is the teaching of our Most Honored Father and that, perhaps, he owes the great blessings he has received from God to this holy practice.

In his goodness, the Count will often speak freely with you; be careful to show respect always and to be reserved in your speech. Above all, my dear Sisters, if God should allow some small disputes between you, never mention the matter to him nor to anyone else. And, if you have grounds for complaint among yourselves, never allow it to appear on the outside.

It is most necessary that you never say anything rude to one another, especially in front of externs. With the help of God, your charity will prevent your being unpleasant with one another.

The close union that should exist between you shall be maintained by mutual forbearance with one another's failings and by the account you give of what you have done, where you have gone, or where you are going during the day. When some difficulty arises in your exercises, for example when the sister in charge of the sick, or she who is in charge of the children experiences some doubt, you shall talk it over together. As soon as you have found a solution, both of you, if possible, shall discuss it with the Count or with the Superioress, if there is one.

You are to conduct yourselves simply, according to the practice common to Paris and other places. However, if someone wishes you to act otherwise, you shall follow their orders so long as they are not offensive to God. Recall the same practice of our Most Honored Father who believes that the advice of others is always worth more than his own.

One of the great needs of our sisters is that they satisfy the people, and in this way God will bless their work and it will result in His Glory. This need is encountered everywhere, but especially here where the people are extremely fond of the hospital. Great gentleness and cordiality are necessary in order to win over these people. That is why it would be well if every morning each sister would individually pray (so as not to multiply the prayers said under the Rule) for the blessing of our good God in order that they might act in the manner of His Son while he was on earth as they carry out the works of charity to which they have been called. Better yet, they should pray that the same Spirit that acted in Him should act through them. They should begin their day by reflecting that they are accompanied by Jesus Christ, the Blessed Virgin and their guardian angel. It would also be well to have devotion to the guardian angels of all the souls in the city.

Our sisters shall be mindful to show great respect to priests, particularly to the chaplain of the hospital to whom they should show no familiarity. If necessity requires them to speak to him, they shall always do so together or in the company of another person. They shall take the parish priest as their confessor, believing that they will always find a blessing in remaining obedient.

As for your conduct toward the sick, may you never take the attitude of merely getting the task done. You must show them affection; serving them from the heart; inquiring of them what they might need; speaking to them gently and compassionately; procuring necessary help for them without being too bothersome or too eager. Above all, you must have great care for their salvation, never leaving a poor person or a patient without having uttered some good word. When you meet someone who appears quite ignorant, have them make acts of faith, contrition, and love; for example: "I believe all that the Holy Church believes, and I wish to live and to die in this faith." At other times, it would be well to have such persons recite separately the principal articles of our faith.

They shall not forget to give a report of the expenditures for their trip and any money remaining to the Count. If they are housed separately, either in or outside the hospital, their expenditures are to be taken care of by the Count and kept separate from other accounts. If they are also required to spend money for the poor, one of them should handle these funds and the other, the money of the poor.

If, as is the custom in the parishes of Paris, you were to receive an annual sum, it would not be necessary to give an account of your expenditures to the Count. However, since he sets no limits and money is requested as needed, you must furnish him with separate accounts of expenditures both for yourselves and for the poor.

As for your food, you may not change it even if you are offered better than that which you receive where you are housed.

Our sisters shall remember to be as recollected as possible in all places, visiting no one and allowing no one to enter their quarters, whether to visit or to engage in useless conversation.

When they are requested to do something the propriety of which they doubt, they shall defer the matter as long as they can in order to have the time to seek the advice of the Superioress.

Our dear Sisters are most humbly requested, at the beginning, to send us news every two weeks, and to pray for us and for the entire Company. On our part, we shall often implore God to grant them the blessings they need for the fulfillment of His will. May He be eternally blessed.

A.14b   To the Virgin Mary

Most Holy Virgin, you know the emotions of my heart today at the thought of your Divine Son in the Crib and how great this mystery seemed to me when I considered that it was the introduction of the law of grace granted to all mankind, which until then had been held captive by the guilt of original sin, that deprived all souls of the vision of God for which they had been created.

O holy time of grace! Why are our souls not in a continuous state of joy and happiness? Why does this

135

time not suffice to fill our lives with love for so good a God?

O my God, I wish to reflect often upon this and to recognize Your infinite mercy because You created me. After this holy time, I beg You to make me most grateful for this favor.

Most Holy Virgin, how admirable is your virtue! You are the Mother of God, yet you did not disdain to live in humility and poverty. You did so to confound our pride and to make us esteem the grace of God above all worldly splendors, which are truly worthless in comparison.

O my God, why am I unable to reveal to the world the beauty which You have shown me as well as the dignity of the Blessed Virgin? Everything is comprised in her title of Mother of the Son of God. How admirable are her deeds! With good reason the Church addresses her as the Mother of Mercy because she is also the Mother of Grace.

I gaze upon you today, most pure Virgin Mother of Grace, since it was you who not only provided the matter for the formation of the sacred body of your Son, at a time when you were not as yet actually a mother, but by bringing Him into the world, you have become both Mother of God and Mother of the Man who at His birth brought a new law to the world, the law which alone leads to eternal life. You are the Mother of the Law of Grace because you are the Mother of Grace incarnate. It seems to me that I have never looked upon you as such. If the people of Israel held Moses in such high esteem because they had received the revelation of the will of God through him, what love and service must I not render to you for having brought the God of the Law of Grace into this world. I shall manifest my gratitude to you by the praise I offer, by my zeal in helping others to recognize your greatness, and by renewed devotion and trust in your powerful intercession with God.

Help me, I implore you, most Holy Virgin, to put such appropriate resolutions into practice.

A.20 (Thoughts on the Cross)

Weeping, Saint Paul exclaimed that many persons living in the world are enemies of the Cross of Jesus Christ.

Consequently, we are called upon to honor this Holy Cross by all types of suffering, after the example of Our Lord, who teaches us this by His death on the Cross and by all the other pains and sufferings which He endured during His life on earth and which are recounted in several places in the Gospel. But souls chosen by God are very particularly destined to suffer, and this is such a sweet and agreeable privilege for them that they would rather die than not suffer since they consider loving and suffering as one and the same thing.

Our Lord wanted us to understand the dignity of suffering when He told Saint Paul that he would be honored by the privilege of suffering in His name. This belief is a truth which must be deeply rooted in our hearts. Effectively, what are we accomplishing on earth when we suffer? We are applying to ourselves the merit of the sufferings of Jesus Christ.

And what is God doing in heaven? He is eternally fulfilling the purpose for which His Son suffered and died, by granting eternal happiness to souls redeemed by this Divine Savior.

O Holy Cross! O suffering! How amiable you are since you are honored and will be eternally honored because of the power which you have given souls to praise and love God!

O Holy Cross! O suffering! How amiable you are

since the love of God has given way to you in His Son to gain through you the power to give paradise to those who had lost it by pleasure!

A.36 (Thoughts on the Feast of Saint Fiacre)

Saint Fiacre left his country and the house of his father, the King, in order to live in the desert of Brie. This generous action could have been prompted only by a strong interior grace which, at one and the same time, enlightened his understanding and revealed to him the greatness of God and the contempt that he should have for all the splendors of the earth.

Grace thus touched his will and penetrated the depths of his heart, removing from his soul any obstacle to the dispositions which God in His goodness was giving to him. In order to make him a perfect man, God so filled him with His divine love that he left everything so as to possess the plentitude of this love.

At the sight of this divine action, I prayed that God would act in a similar manner in my soul and remove from it any obstacle to the grace which His goodness willed to bestow upon it and fill it with the necessary dispositions. I then resolved to cooperate and to strive to rid myself of the evil inclinations that often lead to sin, which is nothingness opposing itself to the omnipotence of God. I shall make every effort to avoid idleness, which is of such great importance because it imprisons the soul in a state of vicious poverty, since every instant that the soul cooperates with God it can amass immense treasures.

Not only did Saint Fiacre leave his country, but he did so in order to avoid becoming its King. When the emissaries of his father's kingdom were pursuing him, he begged God to cover him with leprosy so that they would leave him in peace in his hermitage.

As I reflected on the life and plans of Saint Fiacre, I saw that by renouncing his kingdom he took over the rule of a much more important one because it is said that each human being is a microcosm of the universe.

Therefore, I looked upon him as the peaceful possessor of his little republic, overcoming, or rather, having overcome, his passions by the repudiation of all worldly pretentions. At the moment of death, friends and pleasures forsake those who have pursued them, but the subjects of our spiritual King will never abandon Him because they have been transformed from worldly, temporal, and sensual beings into celestial and spiritual ones.

What a happiness it is to contemplate such a soul ascending to Paradise! There the King of kings will welcome triumphantly this Prince and his court and make him one of His principal courtiers. I hope to imitate him by willingly renouncing everything and especially by placing no value on any position of authority and by trying to be relieved of office prior to my death, or, rather, during my lifetime. Neither shall I be concerned about who will replace me when business calls me away since I must believe that God is to be the absolute Master in the direction of souls.

I did not feel up to traveling. However, I asked God for good health because I had been advised to do so but, desiring to imitate the sentiments with which Saint Fiacre prayed for leprosy, I implored God not to cure me if I was not going to make a similar use of my restored health. I prayed also to be rid of all useless suspicions concerning my neighbor.

Our meditation on pilgrimages caused me to reflect that, in creating souls, God placed them here on earth as pilgrims destined to be in the company of their bodies only for a time. I considered that the greater number of our forefathers did not possess a permanent home and often undertook pilgrimages of devotion, perhaps to place before their eyes the fact that this earth was not their true home. In order to convince them of this truth, it often pleased God to have them accompanied by angels. In imitation of their example, I should willingly accept any change of place that Divine Providence may allow, being accompanied interiorly by my guardian angel.

I also thought that our first father, Adam, wanted to perpetuate his life on earth, in opposition to the plans of God, by eating the forbidden fruit and that, instead of acquiring life, he met with death. So as to remedy this evil, the Son of God came in person as a pilgrim, His life being one unending pilgrimage. This should be the example for our lives. Therefore, I have resolved to meditate profoundly on His life and to try to imitate it. I spent a great deal of time reflecting on the title of Christian which we bear, and I came to the conclusion that we must, indeed, truly conform our lives to the life of Our Lord Jesus Christ. In order to do this, I thought that I should study the manner in which I had acquired this name and the words employed by Holy Mother Church in conferring it upon us. Finally, I must remember that I received this holy name so as to become a true Christian.

A.42 (On the Multiplication of the Loaves in the Desert)

Cum sublevasset oculos

This action of Our Lord as man must reveal the modesty of His exterior demeanor to us. It also permits us to understand that as God His divine gaze is the continual safeguard for the preservation of our natural and immortal being. Likewise, this benign gaze protects the grace which subsists in us by His love and goodness alone. Therefore, I must be eternally grateful to Him for this as well as for his mercy which He shows us in all the actions of His holy life and particularly in the care that His Providence wills to have for the flocks which follow Him. As if He were ignorant of a way to provide for their necessities, He asks where bread can be bought.

O my God, you desire to teach me the means for obtaining Your help in my needs. By the powerlessness which appears in this place, I see that I must admit my lowliness and recognize the truth of my nothingness in order to draw down upon me the greatness of Your mercy.

O Holy Providence, You are the source of all these graces! Grant, I beseech You, that I may confide my soul to You forevermore. It is by the loving gaze of Jesus upon me that I shall obtain this grace. However, this gaze comes from above. Therefore, with the help of His holy grace, I shall detach myself from the earth and attach myself closely to God. By the practice of His Holy Presence, this gentle gaze will inflame me with His holy love.

As the deer seeks water, so my soul seeks God. I shall prepare myself by a great desire to be united to Him so that, as food shares its properties with the human body which consumes it, so the union of my soul with God may render it conformable to Him, and the reception of the Precious Blood of my Savior may lead me to imitate His most holy life.

A.71 (On Holy Communion)

(August 18, 1647)[36]

The Conference on Holy Communion treats of two points. The first point deals with the reasons why we should give ourselves to God to communicate worthily.

It appeared to me that there are two principal reasons in which all the others are comprised, one is the fear and the other the love of God.

141

The precept of the Church binding us to go to Communion once a year under pain of mortal sin shows that it is God's absolute will for us to communicate. It would seem from this threat that we should go to Communion frequently under pain of losing many graces which would be given to us in Holy Communion. It also behooves us to give ourselves to communicate worthily because, if we do not do so, we shall be in danger lest the threats addressed both to those who do not go to Communion at all and to those who communicate unworthily be levelled at us in punishment for our sins.

The other reason that we have for giving ourselves to God to communicate worthily is the gratitude we should have for the great love which He reveals by giving Himself to us in Holy Communion. We can only do so by testifying a reciprocal love of Our Lord, by desiring with all our heart to receive Him since He wishes with all His heart to give Himself to us. His love appeared to me to be all the greater from the fact that, His Incarnation having sufficed for our Redemption, it would seem as if He gives Himself to us in Holy Communion solely for our sanctification, not merely by the application of the merits of His Incarnation and death, but also by the communication which His goodness desires to make to us of all the actions of His life, and to establish us in the practice of His virtues, desiring to make us like unto Himself by His love.

On the second point which deals with what we should do in order to give ourselves to God to communicate worthily, it seemed to me that we should have a high esteem of Holy Communion, that such an esteem inspires a fear in us of not having the dispositions for communicating worthily and that, as one of the effects of Holy Communion, and the principal one, is union with God, we should strive, as far as it is in our power, to remove all hindrances to this union. And as the most dangerous of all is to be too self-centered and self-willed, through love of our own will, it is essential for us to give ourselves to God to have only one will with Him if we are to participate in the fruits of Holy Communion. This is what I desired after I had been taught by God, on so many occasions, that I am incapable of any manner of good and utterly unworthy of Holy Communion.

It seemed to me that I should regard more attentively the actions of the Son of God in order that, aided by His grace, I may unite mine to His.

Because I know that God sees all things, I think I should always have a right intention when I go to Communion, without any admixture of human respect, and go solely for the love I should bear the holy and divine humanity of Jesus Christ, so that I may faithfully correspond to the love He bears me in this most Holy Sacrament. The knowledge God has imparted to me of the many occasions when, in the course of my life, I abused Holy Communion, by leading a life which rendered me unworthy of It and by the violence of my passions, inspired me with a desire to mortify them, so that I may not incur God's hatred instead of His love, if I continue to make a bad use of this divine Food.

A.63   (Reasons for Persevering in One's Vocation)[37]

Three reasons why the Daughters of Charity must have the firm resolution to remain in the Company all their lives:

The first is the esteem we must have for the grace of our vocation.

The second is the danger to be found in uncertainty which causes us to think constantly of the future and which prevents us from making good use of the present.

The third is the occasions which the Daughters of Charity will constantly encounter for losing their vocation.

Means for making and keeping this resolution
The first is to ask God earnestly for the grace to do so.

The second is to reflect often on this vocation both as coming from God and as received by us, always recognizing our unworthiness.

The third is never to allow any thought which might lead us to abandon it.

Signs by which we may know those sisters who have taken such a resolution
The first is to be exact in the observance of her Rules.

The second is to encourage the other sisters and to have a great desire for the perfection of all.

The third is to show great cordiality and to give proof of strong and respectful friendship.

A.68 (On Obedience)[38]

(August 7, 1650)
The first reason that occurred to me is that God, in creating the world, has subjected all creatures to obedience and in such a manner that it seems to me it was only His reasonable creatures who contravened His command and that this obliges us to love and practice obedience.

Another reason is that disobedience has always been so displeasing to God that when disobedience was introduced into the world by man, it was necessary for one of the three Persons of the Blessed Trinity to become Man, not only to let us see by His acts of obedience how reasonable it is for us to obey, but also that our imperfect acts of obedience might, by being united to those of the Son of God, acquire the merit of His, and this is a very strong motive for acquiring and practicing the virtue of obedience.

A third reason is that without obedience there would be continual disorder in every family, especially in Communities, and particularly so in that of the Daughters of Charity, both on account of the freedom of going to different places afforded them by their mode of life and by the interior and exterior disorder that would be caused by disobedience.

And as obedience may be observed in different ways, it seemed to me that, if it is to be such as God demands of me, it is essential to obey with great simplicity and humility.

Secondly, we should obey those who have a right to command, without making any distinctions, and as if it were God Himself who commanded since it is for love of Him that we should obey and do His holy will.

A third condition of true and meritorious obedience is not to influence our Superiors to order us to do what we ourselves desire but to strive that we may be ordered to do what they know God demands of us.

In the fourth place, I think that obedience should be cheerful, prompt, and uncritical, with submission of our own judgment and a faithful observance of whatever we may have been ordered to do. It will help us very much, in my opinion, if we accustom ourselves not to be self-opinionated and to yield to all sorts of persons, even in trifling matters.

I felt deeply ashamed, for I saw that I have frequently failed in all those observances through my pride and obstinacy, of which I repent and ask pardon of all my sisters who may have remarked it.

One of the means which I thought might help me

to acquire this virtue of obedience, such as God demands it of me, is to esteem it highly; frequently to call to mind the obedience of the Son of God in matters that are painful and difficult for us; to reflect that it was His will that obedience should be observed even unto death and that this was to help us as an example and an encouragement.

Another means I hope to make use of is to be on the lookout for opportunities for practicing obedience. If I am not fortunate enough to have them frequently in my daily life, I thought that I should bear in mind, whenever I give orders or suggestions to those to whom I am bound to do so by my office, that it is because I have been commanded to do so by the will of God expressed to me by my Superiors.

A.44b   Formula of the Vows[39]

I, the undersigned, in the presence of God, renew the promises of my baptism, and I vow poverty, chastity and obedience to the Venerable Superior General of the Priests of the Mission in the Company of the Daughters of Charity in order to give myself, for the whole of this year, to the corporal and spiritual service of the sick poor, our true Masters. I shall do this with the help of God which I ask of Him through His Son Jesus Crucified and the prayers of the Holy Virgin.

A.11   Notes During a Retreat

I began my retreat with so many occasions to mortify my judgment that I wonder if this has not caused the interior suffering that I am now experiencing. These contradictions led to painful dryness in my customary prayers which lasted a long time, and I was very close to murmuring.

The refusal to send a sister to Madame Manceau, believing that this was an honest decision and for her good. The decision to let another sister go to a place near her own home.

Finish the reading.

What a remedy for activity is to be found in recognizing my faults, reflecting on them, and grieving for each of them as well as for the shortcomings of the entire Company.

Am I mistaken when I think that I clearly perceive the interior motives of others, particularly my sisters in the Company?

I wonder if my idiotic behavior in revealing myself and in seeking advice is not putting me in danger of perdition. What prevents me from stopping, so it seems to me, is my inability to find the proper words to express what I really mean.

Did I fail in refusing the women of Saint-Etienne? Am I satisfying some passion on the occasions when I feel a certain repugnance in doing what I believe I must do?

Must I refrain from so much exterior dissipation in the use of elegant phraseology when speaking so as to expedite matters?

Should there be adaptations in my mental and vocal prayers and in my Rule?

Should I continue the prescribed reading in *Grenade* and in the New Testament?

Reflections on the little occasions for amusement that I find in holy cards and other devotions.

The pleasure I find in children. My conduct when there is something in the House belonging to them which is not in customary use. I pay for these things according to their market value rather than their actual worth.

In order to practice obedience, reflect on the Communion of union.

To supplicate very humbly that, for the love of

God, I be warned of my faults since this could no longer hurt me. I seek also to be advised of the failings of the Company for the glory of God. I am certain that His goodness will grant me the grace to make good use of these admonitions.

M.20b Love of God the Creator
The love which God has for our souls proceeds from the knowledge that He has of the excellence of the being which He has given to them and which participates in His life. This knowledge enables us to recognize their greatness since it is an act outside of God equal to the one which He produced in Himself when He begot the Second Person of the Godhead. However, since our souls are not God Himself and since His knowledge produces the love which He has for them, may He deign to take fatherly care of the general well-being of those who are completely resigned to the designs of His holy will.

M.40b Abandonment to Divine Providence
I must practice great humility and mistrust of myself; abandon myself continuously to the Providence of God; imitate, insofar as I am able, the life of Our Lord who came on earth to accomplish the holy will of God His Father; assist my neighbor to the best of my ability both corporally and spiritually for the love which God has for all of us equally; carry out my spiritual exercises carefully.

A.14 Thoughts on the Incarnation and the
Holy Eucharist
The Son of God took a human body in the womb of the Blessed Virgin in a state of innocence more perfect than that of the first man. This action was sufficient to satisfy divine justice for the obedience of

our first parents and to reveal to us the truth of the plan of God expressed in the words, "My delight is to be with the children of men."

Nevertheless, this did not satisfy His great love for us. He desired an inseparable union of divine nature with human nature. He accomplished this after the Incarnation by the admirable institution of the most Holy Sacrament of the Altar in which the fulness of the divinity dwells continually in the Second Person of the most Blessed Trinity. This union is a means for uniting the Creator to His creature. However, all do not participate in this mystery because free will enables man to bring about his own damnation by following his evil inclinations and the temptations of the devil, or to earn his salvation by grace which applies to him the merits of the Son of God.

We have reason to believe that the assurance which Our Lord gave us that He would always be with us was designed to sanctify souls by means of this continual, albeit invisible, presence and by the application of the merits of His actions to those of His creatures. Our Lord does this either by asking pardon of His Father so as to wash away the sins which we have committed in opposition to the virtues which He Himself practiced, or by rendering the virtuous deeds which men accomplish by the power of His grace pleasing to God by uniting them to His meritorious actions. It seemed to me that it is in this way that the holy humanity of Our Lord is continually present to us. He is among us by the application of His merits and by the sanctification of souls. His presence is like air without which the soul is lifeless. It is thus that I see the Redemption of men in the Incarnation and their sanctification by means of this union of man with God in the person of His Son and by this continual presence, whereby His merits are applied to each soul joined to the personal union of a God to man. All of nature is thereby honored since it causes God to see His image in all mankind, if it has not been disfigured by the refusal of the application of the merits of His Son which sin alone can effect.

This thought came to me after a long period during which I prayed for a great love for the humanity of Our Lord as a means for moving me to practice His virtues especially gentleness, humility, forbearance and love of my neighbor in order to overcome the sins which I so often commit against them.

M.33   Devotion to the Blessed Virgin

All truly Christian souls should have great devotion to the Blessed Virgin, especially in her role as Mother of God. They should honor her, also, because of the virtues with which God endowed her for accomplishment of His holy designs.

Her eminent dignity obliges us to honor her in some way each day. The best way to do this is to unite ourselves to the Church, especially at those times which it has set aside for the express purpose of paying homage to Mary. We should rejoice with her and congratulate her for the choice which God made of her by uniting His humanity and His divinity within her womb. We should also implore her to assist us to preserve in our own hearts a close union with God.

When we are filled with gratitude for the graces that God has bestowed upon us through the Incarnation and the exemplary life of Jesus Christ, let us look upon the Blessed Virgin as the channel through which all these benefits have come to us and thank her by acts of love.

Let us take our Lady as the model for our daily lives and bear in mind that the best way to honor her is by imitating her virtues. We should particularly honor her purity since we are the spouses of Jesus Christ. We should also imitate her humility which led God to do great things in her. Following the example she gave us by living apart from her parents as a very young child, we must be detached from all things. In all of our actions, let us practice these virtues, of which Mary has given us the example, and beg her to offer them to her Son in our name.

Let us celebrate, in a special way, the Church feasts honoring Mary and meditate, during the day, on the mystery proposed. Each day, let us implore her to help us to render to God the service we have promised Him and to be as submissive as she was in accomplishing His holy will.

We should faithfully recite, each day, those prayers which we have chosen to honor her. These should include acts of love as well as of joyful praise for the glory that is hers in heaven. Finally, let us continue to hope that we will one day be with her and will thus be able to render to her all the honor due to her in the divine plan.

A.23 Thoughts on Baptism

Since the sacrament of Baptism is a spiritual birth, it follows that He, in whose name we are baptized, is our Father and that, as His children, we must resemble Him. Consequently, we who are baptized in Jesus Christ are baptized in His death. Thus, our entire life should be a continuous death, for it would be quite prejudicial to the soul to live amidst delights. Moreover, this death in which we are baptized is the result of the love which Our Lord has had for us from all eternity. He could have found no better way to show us that love than by His anticipated death, for if human beings place such a high value on this life that they prefer it to all else, how much greater reason would our dear Master not have had to prize His since He possessed every virtue and had a body in perfect condition? Thus, as the good daughter I desire to be, I want to imitate this good Father. In order to be truly the daughter of death, I resolve, with the help of His grace, no longer to fear that death which will unite us to Jesus Christ for all eternity. It is not logical for the members to flee that which their Head so ardently desired.

Let us live, therefore, as if we were dead in Jesus Christ. Henceforth, let there be no further resistance to Jesus, no action except for Jesus, no thoughts but in Jesus!

May my life be solely for Jesus and my neighbor so that, by means of this unifying love, I may love all that Jesus loves, and through the power of this love which has as its center the eternal love of God for His creatures, I may obtain from His goodness the graces which His mercy wills to bestow upon me.

A.74 (Thoughts on the High Esteem Which We Should Have for Our Sisters)

(January 5, 1651)[40]

The Conference is on the high esteem which we should have for our sisters so as always to speak well of them.

1. On the first point, I thought that one of the reasons which we have for giving ourselves to God to do this is the great difficulty which our love for our own esteem always opposes to the practice of this virtue because of the blindness which it causes us in our own regard and with regard to our neighbor. This often leads us to judge the intentions and actions of our sisters other than they really are.

2. Another reason is that, if we no longer live for ourselves and are truly given to God to acquire this

152

virtue, His goodness will not permit us to abuse the passions which are part of our nature. Rather, God will grant us the grace to act only as belonging to Him by His spirit, and He will not allow us to dishonor this spirit by acting contrary to it since, being entirely His, we cannot go against it.

The second point deals with the faults which we can commit against this holy practice. One is not to have a high regard for it. Another is not to consider the great good that can come from it. The most serious would be to fail to realize that it is very pleasing to God and not to bother to strive to acqure it.

It follows that, if we do not speak well of our sisters when we are together, we will inevitably say something damaging to them or talk about frivolous things. This could be very prejudicial to the Company and scandalize our neighbor who might hear of it.

Another great evil which is to be feared is that we would live together in discord; that we would not love one another enough; and finally, that God would frequently be offended. If we acquire the practice of esteeming and of speaking well of our sisters, a spirit of union, gentleness, and true charity will grow in the Company in keeping with the plan of God when He formed it.

One of the means to attain this virtue is to strive to have a clear understanding of ourselves by awareness of our usual faults.

Another is always to separate the little faults which may appear in our sister from the person committing them. We should always suspend our judgment and excuse her hasty reactions as we would want others to excuse ours. Thereby, we support one another for the love of God.

Another means is to help one another to acquire this habit of speaking well of our sisters. If by chance we should meet a sister who should forget herself so far as to say something unkind about her sister, we should mortify ourselves and refuse to listen. Then we should gently say to her, "My dear Sister, let us remember the admonition which we have received always to speak well of one another."

But the surest means is to humble ourselves; to recognize that of ourselves we can never attain this virtue; and to implore it confidently from God for His glory and love.

A.60   (Obligations of the Servant of the Poor)

The first reason that should cause us to desire to be instructed on the manner in which the Sisters of Charity should act, in all the places where they are employed for the service of the poor, is the danger they are in of doing just the opposite if they do not know how to behave.

— The second is the danger that, by acting otherwise, they will go against the will of God.

— The third is the danger that God will not derive glory from our employments if we do not act as we should.

— 1. Great faults can be committed if they are not well informed concerning their responsibilities. It takes great temerity for a sister to act without knowing how she should conduct herself.

— 2. There is always the danger of offending God when one is uncertain how to behave.

— 3. This lack of instruction could lead to discord rather than to the union which should exist among them. This is the most damaging thing that could happen to the Company and the most opposed to what God is asking of it.

— 4. The fourth evil is that a sister who does not know how she should act would be in great danger of becoming a source of disedification to persons of the world. Moreover, she would not serve the poor in the spirit of Jesus Christ, and she could draw down upon herself the indignation of God by her repeated faults. Little by little, she would become lax, thereby rendering herself unworthy of the graces of God. This might even cause His goodness to withdraw from her the grace of her vocation. Such great faults might finally lead to the total destruction of the Company.

— It seems to me that the first means to help us to act as true Daughters of Charity is always to be disposed to respond to holy obedience with the view of accomplishing the will of God.

— To be available to go anywhere; to be disposed to be submissive to the sister who will be given to us as Sister Servant; and to do nothing without communicating with her.

— Before leaving for a new mission, to take the firm resolution to do nothing contrary to the rules and maxims of the Motherhouse or of the Company.

— To be faithful neither to give nor to receive news, except when told to do so by the Sister Servant who shall not fail to send it to the Superiors in Paris.

— To be very respectful to the Ladies of Charity and to others employed in the service of the poor.

— Neither to meddle nor to speak with them without the advice of the Sister Servant.

— To be very circumspect in speaking with externs, especially concerning private community matters.

— To be supportive, cordial, and submissive to one another. To preserve the spirit of gentleness and charity.

— This could be done easily if the sisters are as faithful as they should be to the practice of their Rule which should be repeated frequently so that they can learn it by heart. It should be read in places where this can be done.

— In order to accomplish these things, they must have great mistrust of themselves and great confidence in God.

— A practice to be remembered is the thought that if Jesus Christ had not been . . .

A.56 Notes on the Meetings of the Ladies of Charity

It is very evident, in this century, that Divine Providence willed to make use of women to show that it was His goodness alone which desired to aid afflicted peoples and to bring them powerful helps for their salvation.

No one is ignorant of the fact that, to carry this out, God used the establishment of the Congregation of the Mission through the instrumentality of Vincent dePaul. Moreover, everyone is aware that through his work this great benefit spread so far that it is apparent that it must be continued by means of the meetings of the Ladies of Charity where needs will be discussed and where, it seems, the Spirit of God presides.

The power which the Holy Father gave to the aforementioned Congregation of the Mission to establish the Confraternities of Charity is the seed of the fruit which has been produced and which is produced daily not only in France but, we might say, throughout the civilized world.

Was it not by means of this light that the Ladies of the Company of Charity recognized the needs of the provinces and that God gave them the grace to aid these peoples so charitably and so magnificently that Paris has become the admiration of and an example for the entire kingdom?

Were not these holy assemblies at which Vincent dePaul, Superior of the Mission, presided, the means which these charitable Ladies employed in order to determine priorities for the distribution of goods to the poor?

As we all know, Monsieur Vincent furnished honest and charitable criteria to enable them to discover true needs and to provide for them prudently. In all of this, they sought to meet the spiritual as well as the temporal necessities of the poor, thereby giving honor to God in heaven perhaps even now by His divine foreknowledge of the innumerable souls which will one day be with Him.

We clearly recognize these truths. Therefore, it seems to be essential for the Company of the Ladies of Charity of the Hôtel-Dieu to continue its functions, since, from the origin of this noble group, their visits to the sick of this holy hospital have brought such apparent good to the place itself and to the souls who have found the way to salvation there.

Through their ministry, some of the sick poor died a happy death as a result of their good dispositions following a general confession. Others recovered but their confessions led to admirable conversions. The Ladies themselves entered on the pathway to sanctification which is perfect charity, such as that which they have practiced in this place where they have frequently put their lives in danger by their service to the sick. All this has been accomplished by Ladies of noble birth such as princesses and duchesses whom we have seen spending entire hours at the bedside of the sick instructing them in the things necessary for their salvation and helping them to free themselves from the dangers surrounding them.

The truth of what has been reported here would be clearly seen had a record been kept of all of the deeds of the Ladies, known as the Fourteen, who have devoted themselves to these holy exercises in keeping their rank.

If all the good which seems to have been accomplished here is not only useful but necessary, is it not reasonable to ensure its continuation? If, in the plan of God, there were some powerful guarantee that, once peace has been restored, everyone will live a good Christian life; that God will no longer be offended; and that each individual will have a sufficiency, then the necessity for the continuation of the Company, which can only subsist through its Assemblies, would no longer be so urgent to meet needs as they appeared in the past and for which there had been so many assemblies which could also cease.

However, I ask if this general refuge for all countries and nations and this discovery of future needs both in France and elsewhere which are related in these holy meetings do not merit to be continued, although they seem to accomplish so little at the present time. The cloud which somewhat overshadows this light will pass and its rediscovery will lead to the fruits which God desires of His work. To this end, it seems that the Superiors and the other officers, if they seek to continue for the glory of God, would perform an action worthy of their greatness and agreeable to Eternal Charity by seeking the means for having ready access to the advice and guidance of that person whom God has employed for this purpose for as long a time as His goodness sees fit to leave him on earth. This appears to be a simple matter to the person who humbly asks your pardon for the temerity of this advice and for her audacity in saying that this assembly and the other establishments of the Charity can obtain strength from God to remain faithful and to persevere in the primitive spirit of the Congregation of the Mission. See if the good to be gained from this is small!

A.89b Instruction to Three Sisters Who Were Being Sent to Poland

On September 5, 1652, Monsieur Vincent, our Most Honored Father, informed our three sisters who had been chosen to go to Poland that they would leave the next morning. However, Divine Providence caused their departure to be postponed until September 7.

The three sisters were: Sister Marguerite Moreau, Sister Madeleine Drugeon and Sister Françoise Douelle. Our Most Honored Father spoke to them in approximately the following words:

"My dear Sisters, I believe that you are aware that the very virtuous princess, the Queen of Poland, has been urging me for more than two years to send her Daughters of Charity who would establish works such as those she had seen in France. Time was necessary to weigh this call to see if it came from God. There can no longer be any doubt about it since this good Lady has persevered in her desire and has put great pressure on me for the past six months to send her Daughters of Charity.

"O what a happiness, my dear Daughters, to be certain of this call for the entire Company! And what a happiness for you who have been chosen from among so many others in the Company who might do better than you! You should have no doubt of this.

"But, my Daughters, why is this call such a cause for happiness? Here are a few reasons:

"The first is that it is God who is calling you. O what a great vocation it is to be called by God! This is apparent from the complaint which we hear from God concerning persons who want to work in His service when He has not called them. Moreover, does Our Lord not reveal the greatness of a vocation to follow Him when He says to His Apostles, 'You have not chosen me but I have chosen you!' Therefore,

159

you should greatly esteem your vocation. Humble yourselves for this grace, my dear Sisters, and be grateful for it. Humble yourselves at the sight of this astonishing action of God for what would you be, my Daughters, had He not chosen to call you from your poor and lowly state to serve Him? Had you remained in the way of life for which you were destined by your birth, you would be performing the manual labor of poor people just as other village girls do. Who would have shown you any more respect than they show to others of your background? This is why you and I have great reason to humble ourselves. However, our humility should be solid and lead us always to look upon others as better than ourselves."

S.1   (Visitation of a House)[41]

The Conferences to our sisters are ordinarily on points of our Rules.

Advice is given on ways to observe them well; on the virtues of which the Company stands in need or in which it has failed; and also on the manner in which the sisters should deal with their confessors or other responsible persons.

The points to be treated in the Conference are given to the sisters a short time in advance so that they may make their meditation on them.

1. The Sister Servant is a compulsive worker. She even chides others if they show repugnance or unwillingness to comply with her wishes rather than admonishing them or taking the trouble to see to it that her orders are carried out when it is the responsibility of a sister to do so.

She also fails to look after the others and tends to keep to herself because of her melancholy disposition. This could be harmful to the sisters and could even stifle warmth and cordiality had she not been admonished of this fault and helped to overcome it.

2. The Sister Assistant, Sister Claude, is almost the same. She is even a little more melancholy and scrupulous. I believe that no attention should be paid to her scruples and that she should not be allowed to make a general confession. She needs to be pushed to take a little more initiative in aiding the other sisters, either by charitably advising them of their faults or of how they should act or by helping them in their difficulties. She sometimes uses her tenderness for her mother as a pretext for her behavior. However, her mother has no need of her assistance. She also likes to come to Paris.

3. Sister Catherine easily listens to externs and even to the complaints of the sisters when they have little occasions for murmuring or dissatisfaction. She is naturally inclined to be a bit affected and self-indulgent and to have a good opinion of herself. You have to approach her to know her needs. Nevertheless, she is a good soul who mends her ways quickly when she is admonished. She is anything but scrupulous. Rather, she needs to be helped to be more concerned about her faults, particularly those against the Rules.

4. Sister Brigide has an open, simple disposition. She is quite willing to be admonished of her faults. She easily becomes annoyed and shows it, but she calms down quickly after her first reaction which is sometimes too violent.

5. Sister Marguerite is somewhat attached to her own opinion and to what she wants to do. She likes to converse with and listen to externs.

6. Sister Antoinette is a bit haughty and not very exact in obedience because of carelessness. By the grace of God, all her faults are natural reactions and not deliberate.

A.78 (On the Naming of Sister Servants)

The first reason is that if we rely on ourselves the choice we make will be suspect, and we will inevitably be inclined to follow our own whims.

Another reason is that if we are truly given to God, we will seek only His interests, and thus we may hope that we will decide everything according to His good pleasure.

We must pay attention to the information we have on the subject and see to it that the sisters we would like to name have a great love for their vocation and for the practice of the Rule, and that they give evidence of wanting to acquire or of having already acquired the spirit of the Company which consists of humility, simplicity and charity.

Another sign we should look for in them is willingness to be the first to do what they are supposed to teach others, and submission to Superiors which is as great or greater that that of the other sisters.

Total openness is the means which those of us who are called upon to make these decisions should employ if we wish to do it well.

A.99 (Notes on the Organization of the Hospice of the Holy Name of Jesus)

(c. 1653)[42]

Wishing to contemplate the work before God, the thought came to me to look at it in all its stages; namely, its beginning, its continuation, and its completion. We must not think of this as the plan of men, but as a plan inspired by God to be carried out by His servants.

Looking at it in its completion, I perceived it as excellent since it concerns the glory of God in the accomplishment of His most holy will which ordered man to earn his bread by working.

Another end is that persons sheltered there will be helped to become participants in the merits of the life and death of Jesus Christ and thereby to gain eternal salvation as much by the instruction they receive as by the good use they make of their time.

Now, since this is a great undertaking, it is important to lay good foundations so as to build it as perfectly as possible and to make it last.

It seemed to me that we should hope that the first persons chosen would be of great integrity and that they should not necessarily be beggars. For this reason, it would be appropriate, after the selection has been made, to help them to understand the importance of the decision which they have made. There may be persons who are relatively well off who would wish to pass for poor people. If, as I believe Divine Providence will permit from time to time, they are skilled in a trade, they shall be allowed to stay only for six months and in order to teach their craft to others.

So as to avoid complications at the beginning, it seems necessary to accept no married men or women, even if they are childless, since this would be a most difficult situation to encounter. Nevertheless, if some such persons wish to be admitted for a period of time and if they are resolved to cut themselves off from their families, it may be possible, after careful reflection and if God so wills it, to find a few who would help to give a good foundation to this work.

The difficulty in accepting such persons arises from the possible necessity of providing them with a bit of wine or beer.

Since one of the greatest assets of this project is the work which it provides, it is necessary to assign tasks which are useful and productive. An acceptable one would be that of clothmaker. Apart from being productive — the cloth could be used in the House and in other places—it employs many persons and requires little equipment. Bootmakers and shoemakers would also be most useful. Any buttonmakers and muslin workers who are skilled in their trade can put the finishing touches on the products before they are put into use.

Other useful workers are: lacemakers, glovemakers who know how to trim, seamstresses who can take in work from the dressmakers of the city and of other places, and pinmakers.

Having quite enough workers to get the project underway and to keep it going, there is no need to consider the expense that will be incurred for tools and building supplies, nor is there need to be concerned about the difficulty of the skills involved or the problem of securing a location cheaply and easily. Divine Providence provides for all, and skills will be discovered through experience.

Rest assured that there will be very little progress during the first year.

A.79 (Memorandum Concerning the Daughters of Charity of Chantilly)

(1654)

The Daughters of Charity, Servants of the Sick Poor of Chantilly, were obliged to live on borrowed money throughout the year 1653 since, for that entire year they received, in grain and cash, only 77 of the 200 pounds due to them. Therefore, they must be paid the sum of 123 pounds to settle this account.

As of October 24, they have received 61 pounds, 12 sous of the approximately 171 pounds which should have been paid to them by this date for the year 1654. Therefore, 109 pounds, 8 sous are still owed to them. Since the month of October, they have received full payment both in grain and in cash.

Moreover, the rent for their housing has not been paid for four years and it falls due once again on the Feast of Saint Martin. The sum involved is 36 pounds per year. To satisfy this debt their furniture has been repossessed and is about to be sold.

A.62 (Motives Which the Daughters of Charity Have for Giving Themselves to God to Obtain the Preservation of the Company)

(May 25, 1654)[43]

The first reason we have for giving ourselves to God to obtain from His goodness the preservation of the Company for many a long year and, if possible, forever, is to be persuaded, as we are bound to be, that God Himself willed its establishment and willed it in the form in which it now actually exists. And God does not wish His creatures to destroy what He has made.

Another reason is that those who would go against the designs of God by contributing to the ruin of the Company would be the cause of the loss of many souls and would prevent many poor persons from being helped. Such infidelity would put their eternal salvation in danger.

Another thing which would contribute to the ruin of the Company would be, first of all, a desire to alter its customs, because this would, in a way, be to prefer one's own judgment to the guidance of God who knows well enough its future needs.

A second thing which could lead to the ruin of the Company would be to have, on account of our cowardice, little love and esteem for the exercises prescribed in our little Rules.

Another thing which could cause the complete destruction of the Company would be for the sisters to forget what they are, and on account of their long collaboration with the Ladies which gives them the opportunity to handle the money donated for the poor and to live comfortably without worrying about earning their livelihood, to become complacent. This could lead to vain satisfaction and the desire to accumulate goods. Forgetting the obligations of their vocation, they could want to become independent in some places. What would be even worse would be the thought of setting aside some funds so as to carry out this miserable design. Should this contagion touch several members of the Company, there would be reason to fear that the goodness of God would be offended and that the total ruin of the Company would ensue.

The means to prevent the destruction of the Company are to reflect frequently on the grace which God has given to us by calling us to it and to ask Him for the grace to persevere in it.

The final means is to strive to acquire the spirit of the Company through the love which we must have for Our Lord and by the practice of humility, simplicity and true charity.

A.67 (On Mortification)

(January 3, 1655)[44]

I think that one of the reasons which we have for practicing mortification is the necessity of keeping our souls constantly in the state in which they were created. Since they were made in the image and likeness of God, they are disfigured, to a certain extent, when we do not mortify our passions but rather allow them to overwhelm us.

Another reason is that mortification is the life of the soul, just as the soul is the life of the body. If we do not mortify ourselves, our souls will die in the pursuit of passion and will be forever displeasing to God.

We must look to the example of Our Lord, although the passions and sins to be found in us were never in Him.

A third reason is that, if we do not practice this virtue, we will never be able to support one another as we must. Moreover, we will become a source of scandal for the world if we allow ourselves to yield to our first emotions.

On the second point, it seems to me that we must practice this virtue particularly by the frequent mortification of our own judgment and openness to the opinions of others.

We must also mortify our self-will and more willingly condescend to our sisters when there is no prejudice possible to the glory of God.

We cannot place limits on the time which must be devoted to the acquisition of perfect mortification. On the contrary, we must undertake this labor generously for our entire lives since it is a matter of mortifying rather than of killing our passions. These passions remain constantly alive within us. Therefore, we must be continuously vigilant and work to mortify them. In order to do this, it would be well for each of us to take the trouble to ask occasionally for some exterior acts of mortification. Nevertheless, this should be done after we have worked to mortify our interior and anything that we may see in ourselves that is contrary to the little Rules of the Company.

Strict mortification of our curiosity is necessary, especially when the sisters are together. Ordinarily, we are anxious to discover the failings and moods of our sisters and also to relate whatever we have heard. We are even obliged to be careful to mortify the feelings of vindictiveness which can cause trouble among the sisters of the parishes when we allow ourselves to complain of our little occasions of annoyance with one another.

If the Daughters of Charity are to persevere in their vocation and obtain from God the graces of which they stand in need, I believe also that, in general, they must strive continuously to mortify their senses and passions by never allowing them to push them to accomplish the evils which they propose. To this end, they must strive to gain insight into this matter.

I acknowledge my guilt before God for my negligence in assisting our sisters in this task and for my failure to give them the necessary example because of my cowardice, my tenderness for myself, and my sensuality.

A.65 Secretiveness

(February 2, 1655)[45]

The interpretation of the spirit of secretiveness has furnished us with more than one motive for putting us on our guard, for it has made us see that it is a demon hidden in the soul which may do us far more harm than the diabolical possession of the body, for one is concerned with eternal life and the other with temporal life only. Another reason is that if we act by this spirit of secretiveness we extinguish, in a manner, the light which Our Lord came to enkindle in our souls. Another reason is that persons who are moved by this spirit are most annoying and troublesome to those with whom they live, and they run a great danger of the spirit of pride gaining an ascendancy over their imagination so that, because from this motive they have desired to hide themselves from others, although unconsciously, they are so hidden from themselves that they cannot make themselves known; and they are thus prevented from receiving the advice and warnings of which they stand in need.

2

Although there are other types of character who, by natural disposition, find it impossible either to speak out or to explain, nevertheless, I think that passions afford much food for this temptation and especially the passion of pride, which suggests to us not to mention this thing or that lest conclusions be drawn from it, or lest people believe that, because we fell into a fault once, we may be always suspected of it. This does great damage to the soul and inclines it to take the liberty to commit a great many other faults.

Persons who have this fault of not opening up their minds freely to their Superiors, when suffering from any mental troubles or when in need, or when they make their spiritual communications, are in danger of telling lies or of practicing much dissimulation. And this habit may be so strongly formed that they may even yield to it in confession. This spirit of secretiveness, proceeding from the evil spirit, may cause such embarrassment to those who possess it as possibly to lead them to despise the warnings of their Superiors and to pay no regard to the duty of mentioning their difficulties, because they believe their Superiors are interested parties or have been influenced by others. This causes them to seek help or consolation where they should not, and to discover sources of help or consolation that are most dangerous and lead to their destruction. Those who gradually come to accept the maxim of the spirit of secretiveness, being unable to keep their own troubles, or what they know of those of others to themselves, are in danger of communicating their thoughts and feelings unsuitably and to all sorts of persons, which is most prejudicial to their spiritual progress; it leads them to offend God and causes those who listen to them to commit the same faults.

As this spirit is most dangerous and frequently unknown to us, we should often ask Our Lord for light to detect it and, if it is in us, each one of us should fear and distrust herself, lest she should have a share of it. In order to get rid of this spirit, it is necessary, as soon as one feels any difficulty and repugnance in admitting the fact, to have recourse to the Holy Spirit, to ask Him for strength, and overcoming oneself, to admit this reluctance for the love of God. Moreover, if any feel inclined to seek consolation in others, by pouring out their mind to them, they should distrust themselves and, furthermore, if they feel any repugnance at the fact that their Superiors may know what they would like to say or even think, they should fear this repugnance.

S.4 (Council)

(October 5, 1655)

The first three Officers began their meeting by determining to treat of three subjects. The first was that they were to be informed as soon as our three sisters,[46] Henriette, Marie-Marthe and Renée, arrived on foot from Nantes. They were also to discuss the manner in which these sisters were to be received.

The second was to determine who should be sent to Châteaudun to replace Sister Genevieve who would be returning soon. The third was to study together the conduct of the sisters so as to be aware of their failings and of the needs and the overall condition of the sisters of the Motherhouse.

It was resolved that we should welcome our dear sisters with cheerful countenances, manifesting our joy at seeing them without mentioning in any way what had occurred at Nantes either when they arrived or at any later date. We determined also to find out as soon as we had greeted them if they needed to eat or if they wished to retire. Had they, in fact, arrived on foot, they were to be given water, in which fine herbs had been boiled, to soak their legs.

Sister Jeanne from Senlis[47] was suggested for Châteaudun and we decided to send her.

Time ran out so we did not discuss anything more. . .

A.13b (On the Mystery of the Incarnation)

As soon as our first parent had sinned, the goodness of God took pity on human nature and promised to repair the fault by the Incarnation of His Word. This promise was so powerful that, although it did not completely abolish sin because of the freedom which God has given to man, it changed its effect, making it personal.

This promise meant that the whole nature could no longer participate in the fault of an individual because the Person of God was now part of it. Moreover, its effect was immediate for us since, from the instant it was made, the divine plan was accomplished in the mind of God.

O admirable love! O hidden secret! What did You want to do, O my God, when you created man since You were not unaware of his weakness? However, the events had to be as they were, O my Master, to make us understand the effects of Your great love.

Was it not also , O my God, so that Your admirable Incarnation might be the source of the graces of which souls stand in need in order to reach their end? When You created our bodies, You gave us all that we need to feed and cloth ourselves and to experience pleasure. However, the soul, by its nature, could never of itself make use of all these means for its preservation. Neither could it become so closely united to God who is its object since He is inaccessible to all beings except

171

through this most admirable of means which makes God man and man God who, continually present to the soul . . . has made it so like unto Himself that He acts in it as He sees fit, conformably to its needs, in order to enable it to attain its end in keeping with His designs for each individual.

Yes, O my God, I wholeheartedly accept this thought which seems to me to be so in keeping with Your goodness and love. To fail to acknowledge the fact that You want to communicate interiorly with man would be, as it were, to diminish and to be ungrateful for the love which You bring to us.

What! You, who would will the communion of the Saints of the Church Triumphant, Suffering and Militant, and who operate all these marvels, would act like the princes of this earth who must remain withdrawn from others in order to maintain their authority! Oh, it is not so. You who are infinite goodness always want to communicate Yourself. Therefore, I shall be more attentive than ever to Your dear presence. Do not, I beg of You, O my Lord, reject the most unfaithful of Your creatures. I hope for this through Your love. I implore You to share the sentiments which You put into my heart during this little meditation with those who need them so that, by loving and honoring Your holy and amiable presence, they may apply themselves to be attentive to it. Thus, You will not refuse to grant them the graces that You infallibly give to those who hold themselves in the disposition to receive them anymore than the sun distinguishes in shedding its rays on all that is before it.

Now is the time for the fulfillment of your promise. Blessed may You be forever, O my God, for the choice which You made of the Holy Virgin! Did not the devil merit final damnation from Your divinity? It was necessary for Your omnipotence to make use of the

172

weaker sex in human nature to crush his head as Your justice had threatened to do. In order to accomplish this, You used the blood of the Blessed Virgin to form the body of Your dear Son. O admirable goodness! What care You took in carrying out Your plan! How long did You defer it?. . .

A.24   (The Sovereign Dominion of God)

In the one true being of God resides the essence of all the other beings which, in His goodness, He has created. Since all time is dependent upon His eternity, it is only reasonable that we should employ it according to His holy will and for His glory. Everything has been created by Him in the most perfect order; therefore, I shall strive more than I have in the past to live as well-regulated a life as possible. I shall begin this month by honoring the sacred order of creation as it was accomplished by the true and only divinity.

A.25   (The Purity of Love Necessary to Receive the Holy Spirit)

Souls that are truly poor and desirous of serving God should place their trust in the coming of the Holy Spirit within them believing that, finding no resistance in them, He will give them the disposition necessary to accomplish the holy will of God which should be their only preoccupation.

In order to be in a state of receptivity, the soul must imitate the obedience of the Apostles by freely confessing its powerlessness and by detaching itself completely from all creatures and even from God Himself, insofar as the senses are concerned, because the Son of God, who prepared His Apostles to receive the Holy Spirit, did so by depriving them of His divine presence at His Ascension. The Holy Spirit, upon entering souls that are so disposed, will certainly remove any obstacle to His divine operations by the ardor of His love. He will establish the laws of holy charity by endowing them with the strength to accomplish tasks beyond their human powers so long as they remain in a state of total detachment.

The love which we are obliged to bring to God must be so pure that, when we receive His most particular graces, we must hope for nothing other than the glory of His Son. Our Lord taught us this in the person of His Apostles to whom He had promised to send His Holy Spirit when He assured them that He would thereby be glorified.

The soul that truly loves God must seek nothing more. The greatest happiness that it can experience is to cooperate in rendering glory to Him whose ignominious death astounded all mankind. Even if, as God, He did not merit the purity of love which would make Him the unique object of all our affections, we would be obliged to render to His holy humanity a debt of gratitude for the greatness of His love.

Blessed, therefore, are they who help others to fulfill their obligations to Him. Blessed are they whose powerlessness prevents from acting in any other way and who employ the full power of their love so as to make the love of their Master the sole proprietor of their hearts.

A.28 (Thoughts on the Excellence of Our Souls)

The love which God has for our souls proceeds from the knowledge that He has of the excellence of the being which He has given to them and which participates in His life. This knowledge enables us to recognize their greatness since it is an act outside of God equal in some ways to the one which He produced in Himself when He begot the Second Person of the Godhead. However, since our souls are not God Himself, and since His knowledge produces the love which He has for them, may He deign to take fatherly care of the general well-being of those who are completely resigned to the designs of His holy will.

A.37 (Heaven Compared to a Mustard Seed)

Our Lord wanted to make the Kingdom of Heaven accessible to us by comparing it to a mustard seed and thus teaching us how easy it is to gain this kingdom which He has won for us by so much labor and suffering and by His death. We are assured that we shall attain this bliss if we desire it. It would appear that this kingdom is but a desire in this world, for what is smaller than a mustard seed, and what is more insignificant than a desire?

What! O my God, is this bliss, which is the sole satisfaction of the blessed, such a small thing? Do You thus minimize the blood and the life that purchased it? Do You esteem it so little as to compare it to a tiny mustard seed? Nevertheless, I am well aware that this seed contains great strength within itself, both in its capacity to multiply and in the quality it gives to everything that is seasoned with it.

Therefore, I shall strive for the desire for heaven and, once I possess this desire, I shall sow it in the soil of my heart. Then I shall ask my God to enrich this ground with the warmth of His love and to water it with the Precious Blood of my Savior so that this seed may grow to its full perfection.

M.69 (On Recreation)

Recreation must always begin with a reminder of the presence of God and of the equality of all reasonable beings in His eyes, reflecting that the least esteemed by men are perhaps the best loved by God.

Recreation should be regarded as a time allowed by the goodness of God to unite ourselves by means of a sincere communication of thoughts, words, and actions. This time should be used to honor the true union of the three distinct Persons of the Blessed Trinity and the admirable union of the blessed in heaven.

During recreation, conversation should be truly lighthearted and cordial. We should converse with those who are agreeable to us as well as with those we favor less, replying graciously without arguing and without taking offense at what is said, bearing in mind the meekness with which Jesus Christ received the blame for His holy words and actions.

Never make fun of a sister who does not speak well unless you are certain that she does not mind it and that your heart is free from uncharitable feelings. Should you be the target of others' amusement, accept the situation graciously and consider your sisters as better than yourself and, therefore, as better loved by God. Look upon yourself as blessed in the occasion offered you of serving them.

From time to time during recreation, raise your mind to God and recall that you are strengthening your mind and body in their weakness during this period of rest. Because of this, they can be better employed in the service of God, according to your obligations, and they are once again given courage for the work at hand.

During this time of recreation, reflect on the eternal joy that you will have in heaven if, on earth, you love God and your neighbor as He has commanded you. To help you practice the love you owe your neighbor, remember when you are together that the bond of union among you is the Blood shed by the Sacred Heart of Jesus Christ.

Conversation during the time allowed must be in a spirit of great charity, following the example set for us by the Son of God while on earth. You must try to associate with those sisters who bring you the closest to virtue, or with those whom you can help in the same way. Keep yourself interested in others. Do not get angry over the actions of the others, especially over their intentions. Avoid individual friendships since you are obliged to a mutual communication with one another in order to maintain the union which must be preserved in your religious family.

Be amiable with all your sisters. Always respect your Superior whom you must look upon as Jesus Christ on earth. Never criticize her manner of governing even when her orders sometimes appear to be contrary to your views or perhaps far from reasonable. Certainly, with a little patience, you will discover that it is the spirit of God more than the spirit of the Superior that is governing.

Be zealous in defending the sisters who are absent. Let your charity be such that you do not easily give in to rash judgments. Always put yourself in the place of those who are blamed either by reflecting on your own faults or by taking into consideration the power of natural inclinations on a person's way of thinking and the near impossibility of getting rid of a habit. Finally, remind yourself and those with you of your mutual obligations to God if you are all exempt from the fault in question. However, be careful that what you say about others proceeds from a truly Christian heart and not from pretended virtue.

Your conversation should center mainly on subjects which help you to fulfill the obligations of your Rules. You should bear in mind that all other acts are more prejudicial than helpful to you.

A.92 (On the Duties of the Motherhouse)

In the name of Our Lord Jesus Christ.

The sisters entrusted with the duties of the House shall consider themselves doubly obliged to give good example to all the Company, and they shall serve the Company in the same spirit of gentleness and charity that they would bring to the service of the poor if they were so employed, recognizing our Lord in these persons.

The Bell-Ringer

The sister who rings the bell shall have a special devotion to her guardian angel so that he will help her to wake up a short time before four o'clock. She must consider that God will hold her responsible for those who, through her fault, would fail to rise. Likewise, however, with the thought of God's approval, she shall consider that she will share in the merits of the prayers which God will give to those who, with her help, will awaken on time.

After waking up, she shall get dressed quietly and shall make her rounds modestly. In order not to distract or amuse the sisters, she shall only say to them what is necessary to awaken them.

She shall be careful to ring the bell for all the exercises: dinner at eleven-thirty; evening meditation at five-thirty; supper at six o'clock; and prayers at eight o'clock, except on Fridays when she shall ring the bell at seven-thirty.

She must remember not to resemble the bell that she rings. A bell does not go itself to the place to which it calls others. However, since she is the first to summon the other sisters, she must also call herself not only to be the first one in the chapel but also to reflect on where she is going and why.

The Portress

As soon as she is named to her office, the Sister Portress shall give thought to its importance and to the great discretion and reserve that she must exhibit. After having asked God for this grace, she shall implore her guardian angel to assist her; and each time she goes to open the door, she shall try to lift her mind to God.

As far as is possible, she shall not let people ring twice, urging herself to diligence by an act of charity and by the thought that, if God in His mercy should send her to purgatory and then free her for her entrance into paradise, she would be most annoyed to be kept waiting at the heavenly portals.

She shall have the key to the pantry and the responsibility to cut the breakfast bread which should weigh no more than three-quarters of a pound. She shall not give seconds nor more than is necessary to anyone.

It is also necessary that she cut up the bread for the soup and that she cut the slices quite thin so that they soak up the bouillon better. In putting the bread in the soup, she shall be reasonable and shall avoid excess so that there is bouillon for those who need it. The others shall give up some of their bread if there is not enough of it.

In order that there be bread enough for the second table, she shall be careful not to slice it too thickly at the first table. She shall make sure that those in need of more bread are given a little.

She shall collect the soup bowls early, in the event that they must be washed for use at the second table.

She shall have care to remove the serving vessels neatly and shall give what is left over to the Sister Cook. She shall also be sure to prepare the soup for the second table while the other sisters go to the chapel to say the Angelus.

When the sisters have finished dinner, which occurs when the first quarter hour is about to be rung or when the majority of them have finished eating, the Sister Portress shall then be sure to go to ring the bell three times to mark the rising from table, and at the same time, she shall remember to adore the three Persons of the Holy Trinity.

I neglected to say that she shall prepare the soup after eleven-fifteen has been rung, and that she shall always prepare first the soup of the poor while honoring Our Lord in each of them.

She shall also be responsible for cleaning, as early as possible, the courtyard and the entrance way, both inside and outside the House, and the stairs leading from the chapel.

The Sister Portress must recollect herself a little each time she opens or shuts the door so that she conducts herself with great modesty and reserve, while at the same time listening seriously and responding to the point.

When news of the sisters is requested, she shall only answer in regard to their health and shall not say where they are placed. If these persons seem most anxious for news, she shall ask them to wait while she goes to obtain the desired information. For this, she shall address herself to the Directress, or in her absence, to the Sister Assistant.

She must never inform a sister that she has visitors until she has obtained permission to do so. If permission is not granted, she must never inform the sister that she has had visitors. Likewise, no messages may be relayed without permission.

The Sister Portress shall not indulge in curiosity when someone comes in and waits, and she shall never ask for news. If someone wishes to give her any, she shall skillfully avoid it. However, if she cannot prevent herself from hearing it, she shall not make it a topic of conversation with the sisters unless it is a matter requiring prayer, in which case she shall notify the Directress or the Sister Assistant.

In the evening, she shall be most careful to close all the doors and windows in the rooms for which she is responsible, and to take the keys to the Sister Assistant.

She shall always have great care to carry the keys with her, never leaving them in the door nor anywhere else, keeping the door doubly locked. When she is requested to do something else, she shall not hand the keys to another sister without the permission of the Sister Assistant or the Directress.

Ordinarily, she shall serve at the first table, and she shall make sure that there is no noise in the refectory. In order to promote this, she shall keep the doors closed and shall not allow in any dogs, cats, or chickens. She shall make no noise, opening and closing the doors quietly. She shall be certain that the sisters lack nothing, such as water and bread, dishing out servings reasonably and without showing favoritism. She shall do all of this mindful that she is serving the servants of Our Lord and the poor.

The Cook

The Sister Cook shall go to the kitchen at exactly six o'clock, or a little before, in order to light the fire and place the pot for the sisters' meal over it. She shall think of the joy that St. Martha and St. Joan of Cusa experienced in preparing food for Our Lord when they were so fortunate as to offer Him their hospitality. Through this thought, she shall move herself to devotion, while considering that she is serving Our Lord in serving His servants in the person of the poor.

She shall do her utmost to prepare the food tastefully so that her effort will compensate for the delicate morsels eaten in other Communities.

She shall be careful to have everything ready for dinner at eleven-thirty, and for supper at exactly six o'clock. For fear that our sisters might be interrupted in their reading — which she herself shall try to hear — the Sister Cook shall make sure that there are no loud voices in the kitchen, nor noises of any kind.

Since the head Sister Cook is also in charge of supplies, she shall be as careful to give the sisters what they need as to avoid superfluity; charity demanding the former and the virtue of poverty the latter. When she becomes aware that any sister finds the food disagreeable or distasteful, she shall charitably give her something better and something which she judges in keeping with her infirmities. Likewise, she shall give them a little something along with the breakfast bread, and shall provide collations for those who are truly in need of them.

This sister stands in need of great charity and prudence so that she does not give more to one than to another. She must consider solely her obligations which should incline her to love and to treat all the sisters alike when providing for their needs. If she is aware that a sister, through temperament, feels that she should receive something different from what she is getting, she shall inform the Directress in order to determine whether or not this sister should be satisfied. But whether she gives or refuses, she should always do so gently and with gracious words.

When the sisters are actually ill, it is then that she must redouble her care in making good bouillons. She must remember that it is the exactitude with which she prepares them rather than the quantity of meat used which makes the bouillons pleasing to the patients.

In preparing the soup, she shall be sure always to save some bouillon to give to the sick sisters in the evening.

Although she must do her best in preparing the sisters' food, she should not use spices except when necessary and then only sparingly. Likewise, she should not use onions since they are most unhealthy for the girls.

She shall do her utmost always to eat dinner at the second table with the sisters rather than alone so as to avoid charges of selecting the best meat for herself. Although she is most diligent in carrying out her duties, she is strongly urged not to become saddened or upset by the complaints that a few of the sisters might make about her. Whether these malcontents accuse her of having prepared too much or too little, of having prepared the food badly, or of having prepared better for herself than for the others, she shall make good use of such murmurs. She shall endure them patiently and console herself with the thought of the countless times that murmurs were issued against Our Lord as He was serving His neighbor. He rejoiced at these times and did not feel guilty.

All the sisters are warned against entering any work area or taking anything from these areas without the permission of the Sister Officers. Likewise, however, the Sister Officers must be gracious to those who approach them for permission. If they are obliged to refuse entrance to someone, for example to a sister who wishes to chat or warm herself in bad weather, they shall do so gently while pointing out to her the importance of obedience. However, whenever they are able to allow the sisters entrance, they shall do so, whether it be to take some live embers or to take some utensil— provided that it is returned, since it is inconvenient not to find the needed utensil.

The Infirmarian

As soon as one or several sick sisters are placed in the care of the Sister Infirmarian, she shall look upon it as a request from Our Lord. She shall consider herself as called anew to make the same efforts that He made on earth when He cured the sick poor, and she shall honor His efforts through the work of watching over and caring for the sick.

She shall take great care to inform the Sister Pharmacist of all that happens to the sick and of all that they need; and she shall never give them food or remedies without her advice.

She shall be exact in following the schedule for their food and medicine and she shall not give them anything that could harm them even if they request it.

Although she makes every effort to perform her duty well, nevertheless it is possible that her patients will complain about her. In such a case, she shall not appear upset, but should excuse them on account of their illness and anxiety. She shall strive to satisfy their requests if there is a way of doing so without causing a mishap. Should a sick sister, through impatience, speak rudely to her or express discontent, she shall pretend not to hear her or she shall quietly apologize, thus honoring the rebukes addressed to Our Lord by the Jews when He cured their sick on feast days.

Since the Sisters of Charity are obliged to serve the sick poor both corporally and spiritually, in imitation of Our Lord who, in curing, always gave some advice for the salvation of souls, saying to some, "Go and sin no more," giving others to understand that their faith would save them, and speaking many more words of advice, our Sister Infirmarians shall take great care that the sick have great submission to the will of God and great trust in His love. They shall see to it that the sick sisters make good use of their trials, offering them to God in union with those of His Son. They shall have care that the sisters' hope for salvation be in the life and death of Jesus Crucified, that their intention for the future be to serve God better than ever before, and that they have great compassion for the sick poor who suffer so much without either the corporal or the spiritual help which they are given. From time to time, it would be well to say to them, "My Sister, while lying in your bed, do you ever think of the sufferings of our sick poor; how they are so often all alone without any fire, lying on straw without sheets or blankets, bereft of all kindness and consolation? Do you not consider yourself most blessed with the graces that God has bestowed on you?"

The Sister Infirmarian shall be most exact to notice any change or accident which occurs in the patients so that she can notify the doctor or the Sister Pharmacist. Likewise, when she notices the sick becoming weaker she shall give notification so that they may be provided with the sacraments.

The Office of the Sister Pharmacist

Since health is the most precious treasure of life, the sister in charge of the pharmacy must be charitable, prudent, and most careful to prepare her compounds in the proper seasons. She shall spare nothing in order to prepare them well, checking on them from time to time to see that none of them have deteriorated, and she shall keep all her pots and bottles well covered.

If God restores their health, they have truly done their best.

A.93 (Remarks on the Common Rules)

(c. 1656)

— Fifth Article — should something be repeated in this article with the words: "in order to merit, as He did, to enter heaven one day?"

— Eighth Article — obscure — it seems to exclude the sisters of the country parishes from sending their surplus funds to the House. This would be unfair since they are clothed at the expense of the House as are the other sisters. In this same article, so long as there shall be a sister at the House who carries the title of Superioress, it has been judged that the first Sister Assistant shall not be called Sister Servant.

Ninth Article — The ordered sentences are from the Ninth Article, the rest are from the Eighth.

Tenth Article — The expression "the ungrateful": is it not too harsh, and does it not seem to presume that the poor owe gratitude to Sisters of Charity? This should not be since the sisters are most obliged to serve the poor.

In following up the statement on the sacraments, it seems to me that if the sick cling to life and desire to receive Communion and have need of confession, that the sisters should provide for them and even incline them to such devotion.

— Eleventh Article — After the last words, "their desires," add "inclining the Ladies or others, to the best of their ability, to do the most good that they can for the poor."

— Nineteenth Article — Following the statement on the Sister Servant, which position should not exist at the House, add "being in the parishes," or else an Article which makes it clear that the Sister Servant must be considered the Superioress by the sisters with her.

186

— Twenty-first Article — Add, as succinctly as possible, something on the good intentions which they may have.

Twenty-ninth Article — A statement on the Sister Servant is here again, and it should not say that they shall be granted permission by the Sister Assistant — unless the Superioress is absent. For several reasons the Assistants risk the danger of being given too much authority since we are not like religious communities.

Thirtieth Article — Does it not seem to stress unduly the possibility that the Sisters may dislike one another? Often it is simply a matter of some mood, action, or word.

Thirty-first Article — Instead of "aversion" say "discontent."

Eleventh Article on the employment of the day. The reading of the subject for meditation follows the reading of the *Martyrology* because the sisters fall asleep if it is done after prayers. If some time remains until the quarter hour, a sister shall repeat the subject for meditation so that it is fixed in the mind for the next day.

The repetition of the meditation takes place every day after morning meditation.

To the end of this article add that it would be well to fall asleep having some good thought.

I have made these remarks because your Charity has instructed me to do so. The passage on the Sister Servant can be made more clear by adding: "being in the parishes."

I have again learned that the Confessor of Chars[48] often forbids talking to the parish priest, and in several meetings also asks what Father has said. It seems odd that they take advantage of one another.

A.81 (Remarks on the Rule for the Sisters with the Foundlings)

Following the Fourth Article

Would it not be appropriate to draw up two or three meditations on the subject of the service of little children? This would point out to the sisters how pleasing this work is to God and the recompense reserved for those who serve the children well. It would also point out the danger of serving them negligently. Such subjects should be meditated on each month.

After the Sixth Article

In order to promote modesty and purity, as well as good health, the sisters shall not permit the children to get out of bed totally naked, nor to undress totally, nor to go barefoot or bareheaded. Likewise, the sisters shall not comb the children's hair in open areas, such as in the courtyard, nor in their rooms near open windows.

In winter, the sisters shall be on guard that the children do not linger near the fire. Rather, they should be made to play some game in order to warm themselves. From time to time, when necessary, they shall be permitted to warm themselves at the fire.

Also, the sisters shall be watchful year-round that the children do not fall asleep in direct sunlight or in unhealthy places.

After the Twelfth Article

The sisters serving in the rooms of the little children shall try to discipline them with little mortifications or gentle words which encourage them to be good. However, when they remain incorrigible and the sisters feel it necessary to punish them in a different way, they shall notify the Sister Servant who shall take a stick to the children herself, or inform the sisters to do so. In order that this may be done without emotion, the sisters should wait awhile after the children's bad behavior before hitting them, and they shall be very careful to avoid hitting them on the head.

Eigth Article, on the Sister Servant
Following "or otherwise" add "unless they be suited to serve at the House."

Ninth Article
Following the words "and the silence" add "except when their duties require them to do otherwise."

To indicate the time that the litanies of the feast days should begin.

Would it not be necessary also to have particular rules for the duties of the sisters of the Motherhouse such as the Portress, the Bell-Ringer, the Cook and the Clothesroom Sister?

She shall see to it that all the thread and silk is used sparingly; that the children have chores and carry them out; and that whatever is made at the House is sold. Likewise, she shall make sure that the merchants pay for the goods in order to keep an account of the profit for the Lady Treasurer of the Company for these children; and to cook. . .

Following the Nineteenth Article concerning the children add "that all the children who work, up to age sixteen, shall rise at five o'clock in summer and five-thirty in winter. Ordinarily, they all shall go to bed precisely at nine o'clock."

The sister in charge of the children shall be in their room as they rise from bed. She shall take them to the chapel to pray to God, and upon their return, she shall have them recite their lesson. Then they shall begin work and their breakfast shall be brought to them at eight o'clock.

This sister shall take one or two of these children to Mass every day at the time judged most appropriate by the Sister Servant so long as Mass is not said at the hospital. She shall keep the children in front of her while in the chapel and she shall make sure that they pray attentively. Upon their return, she shall reprimand them for any faults committed while in the chapel.

On the Seventh Article of the Rule
Following these words "as soon as they will be gotten up from bed," add "which shall be, at the earliest, at seven o'clock for the very small children, and at six-thirty for those from six to seven years old."

On the Eighth Article
Instead of the Benedicite being said by the sister, she shall have one of the older girls say it, each one taking a weekly turn. Those girls who do not go to Mass every day shall say their Rosary every day, at different times during the day; that is, a decade after morning prayers, two decades after Grace at dinnertime, and two decades after Grace at suppertime.

A.66   (On the Necessity of Accepting Changes)[49]
The first reason that obliges the Daughters of Charity to accept changes of place, persons and duties is the respect that they owe to the example of the Son of God who acted in this way.

The second is that such changes can and must occur. If they are not accepted, we shall never enjoy the peace of soul that is essential if we are to please God and to accomplish His holy will.

The third reason is that the sisters must take into

190

consideration the difficulties that Superiors encounter in trying to please everyone; in finding Daughters of Charity to send to serve the poor in places where they have been requested; in trying to avoid the many inconveniences that may arise.

If the sisters are not willing to accept changes in all these circumstances, they are in danger of committing many faults. If it is a sister who has been changed so that another may be sent in her place, if she is dissatisfied with her replacement or has heard rumors about her, she will not welcome her cheerfully and cordially. No kind words will be exchanged and there would be reason to believe that once they are together they will be in continual disagreement. In such instances, it is extremely difficult not to reveal one's feelings and matters may progress to such a point that, in conversation with the Ladies, the evil spirit might suggest words that are harmful to our sister.

Another evil is the disedification that we would give to our neighbor. Moreover we would find ourselves in the impossiblity of faithfully practicing our Rules and we would be in danger of losing our vocation. There are an infinite number of other evils which would befall us but which are too lengthy to mention here.

A.45   (Advice Requested from Monsieur Vincent)
December 30, 1656

After I had recovered from my most recent serious illness in the month of . . . of the present year, I asked Monsieur Vincent, Our Most Honored Superior and Founder, with what dispositions I should once again take the resolution to live.

In addition to giving me other counsels which were in conformity with the holy will of God, His Charity told me that I should do this with the determination to deny myself any satisfaction and to renounce myself by refusing all that is agreeable to my senses and passions so as to honor the practice of the Son of God in the use that He made of occasions for renunciation. During the illness which followed my fall, I wanted to discover the means that I should employ to help another person to know her faults. I told My Most Honored Father that this desire had led me to point out her failings to her and that I realized that my admonitions appeared to have profited her very little.

His Charity told me that we must put up with a great deal and rely more on God than on our own means. He said, "Pray tell, who are we to think that we can undertake such a difficult and important task?" This remark made me understand that I had been hasty in my zeal and that my own passions had sometimes come into play. It also taught me that I should serve souls in their needs by another practice, that of turning to God by an interior act of confidence and trusting Him to accomplish by His grace and goodness all that I could not do. This seemed to be a more efficacious means.

I then spoke to His Charity of the direction of our sisters with their diverse personalities and employments and the liberty they have because they are in so many different places. In his kindness, His Charity told me, among other things, that direction is a gift which must be obtained through patience. This led me to understand that we must not always let others know that we have noticed their faults. Moreover, we must overcome our repugnances in putting up with them, especially when they are minor, and be careful not to allow ourselves to yield to sudden emotion which might cause us to resolve, in our direction, to rid ourselves of the services of some sisters for whom we must always. . .

A.32 (On the Virtues of the Most Holy Virgin)

Her conception which God made immaculate in anticipation of the merits of the life of her Son.

All the graces infused into her soul because of the choice which God made of her to be His mother.

Her birth; her most pure life dedicated to the service of the Temple; and her vow of virginity.

Her marriage; her submission and dependence; her trust in Divine Providence; her tranquility; the inexhaustible spring of all the virtues of her beautiful soul during her marriage, sustained as she was by her great humility which kept ever before her eyes the work which God was accomplishing in her.

Her complete detachment and the sweet tranquility of her soul during the passion and death of her Son.

Her renunciation of all things and her willingness to remain on earth after the Ascension of her Son because of her pure love of God and her zeal for the salvation of souls, for which she labored for the remainder of her life, thereby imitating perfectly the Spirit of her Son.

I offer You, O my God, all the glory which You will receive forevermore from the beatitude of this most holy soul which You have rendered extraordinarily capable of experiencing the plentitude of Your divinity.

Blessed is this heart filled with love which, by the interior sufferings of her soul, brought death to her body laden with merit.

May her soul, chosen among thousands of millions, be glorified for all eternity because of her total acceptance of the plan of God.

May this precious body, united to so worthy a soul, be forever glorified because of the testimony of love which the Blessed Trinity will show to it throughout eternity.

M.70   (On Confession)

We must open our minds to a true understanding of the sacrament of Penance and weigh very seriously our motives for approaching it. Since this sacrament can be applied only to sinful souls, we must recognize and acknowledge ourselves as such before receiving it. We must also admit that we have rejected the grace of God which is an unbearable evil for the truly Christian soul. Once we are fully aware of our state and realize that confession is the only remedy for our great affliction, we should carefully examine our conscience. We must then conceive a holy hatred for ourselves because we have been so irrational as to oppose God who has always been so good to us and who of Himself merits infinite honor. This self-hatred should lead to filial regret for having offended God and the firm resolution to overcome ourselves and to avoid the occasions which so frequently cause us to fall into sin. Above all, we must recognize that of ourselves we can do nothing to avoid sin and make an act of loving confidence which will move us to ask God for the grace to desire to please Him more earnestly in the future. To this end, we must pray for the grace to avoid even the smallest failings so that we may love God for Himself alone.

Once we have entered into these dispositions, with a heart filled with shame, we should present ourselves at the feet of the priest as before a judge. After accusing ourselves of our sins simply and humbly, we should await absolution in fear and in hope. We should receive it with admiration, reflecting that the great love of God for us has willed that the remembrance of the cruel death of His Son merit pardon for our sins.

A.26 (Reasons for Giving Oneself to God in Order to Receive the Holy Spirit)

1657

The first subject of my meditation is my powerlessness to enter into prayer because of my attachment to myself.

Considering myself as belonging to God because He is God and because He created me, which are the two foundations of His proprietorship over me, I saw that I belonged to Him also because He preserves me. This preservation is the support of my being and a sort of continuous creation. I then asked myself what I intended to do so as to give myself to Him. I saw that His power to possess me was, by the excellence of the divine plan in the creation of the human race, to be found in His close, eternal union with His creatures. He brought this about through the unique means that He possessed which was the Incarnation of His Word. As perfect man, the Son willed that human nature should participate in the Divinity through His merit and through the close union of His nature with the Father. O what wonders are seen in heaven in souls that have given themselves to God in the only way possible, which is by means of the gift of their free wills which they make use of exclusively as belonging to Him!

O excellence of souls that are free, that no longer belong to themselves, of souls that act in all their thoughts, desires, and deeds in conformity with the justice of God, of souls that find nothing so reasonable, so beneficial or so just as to give themselves to God!

What love, what a unique gesture on the part of God, to make known His omnipotence in this unequaled way! He willed His creatures to be so closely united to their Creator that they would be one with Him in matters related to them.

Confusion for failures in this regard— entire oblation — distrust of self— resolution to do better in the future.

Second meditation on the second reason for giving myself to God so as to dispose myself to participate in the reception of the Holy Spirit, which is the loss I would suffer and the harm I would incur if I did not do so.

One of the greatest losses that a soul can experience by not participating in the coming of the Holy Spirit is that the gifts infused at Baptism do not have their effect, which leads us to see the truth of the warning of Our Lord to cowardly and lazy souls that, not only would they receive nothing, but what they have will be taken from them. This means placing ourselves by our misery in such a state of powerlessness that even grace can do nothing for us. Oh, how many times have I been in this condition, thus removing myself from the order of the designs of God, which are great for those to whom He sends the Holy Spirit. This made me realize that all the disorders of life are caused by the failure to give oneself to God so as to receive the Holy Spirit. The lack of these gifts is apparent in the strange difference in comportment between persons who are animated by them and those who are not. The actions of the latter are earthy and unreasonable as is often my case on account of my misery. I have experienced this too often in the disorder of my senses and passions.

What means are to be employed and what dispositions are necessary in order to participate in the reception of the Holy Spirit.

The first one that occurred to me was that Our Lord told His Apostles that He had to leave them so as to return to the Father and to send them the Holy Spirit. This taught me that I must be completely detached from all creatures and even from the Divine Presence so that my soul may be empty of all obstacles and the Holy Spirit may fill it with His presence and gifts which will draw me out of my lassitude by the power of His love and cause me to act by His strength.

Therefore, it is not enough for You, O Lord, to have taught me the means for disposing myself for the coming of the Holy Spirit. I must also labor diligently, O my soul, to remove all obstacles and to act, or better, to let the grace, with which the Holy Spirit wills to fill all the powers of my being, act in me. This can only come about by the destruction of the evil habits which, on diverse occasions, hinder His action in me.

O Eternal Light, lift my blindness! O Perfect Unity, create in me simplicity of being! Humble my heart to receive Your graces. May the power to love which You have placed in my soul no longer stop at the disorder of my self-sufficiency which, in reality, is but powerlessness and an obstacle to the pure love which I must have as a result of the indwelling of the Holy Spirit.

Confusion then for myself because of my errors which have often attached me to falsehood and led me to abandon eternal truth. Consume all that, O Fire of Divine Love, although I do not merit this grace.

The subject of this meditation is a continuation of the preceding one on the means and dispositions necessary in order to participate in the coming of the Holy Spirit.

The first seemed to me to be the esteem that we must have for this gift both with regard to its greatness and to the benefits and the eternal honor that we will derive from it. Is there anything more excellent in heaven or on earth than this treasure? How is it possible to live a disorderly life after having given oneself entirely to be open to this infinite good? Should I not desire, O my God, to die upon receiving it? To live for as long as it pleases You, but with Your life which is one of total love. May I not, beginning in this world, flow into the ocean of Your Divine Being? Should I be so fortunate as to receive the Holy Spirit, oh, how I must desire this with my whole heart!

No longer to walk any path but this one; no other satisfaction but that of loving and of willing Your good pleasure.

You still see weaknesses in me in my desire for the affection of creatures. Consume this, O Ardent Fire of Divine Love! By the power of Your grace, weaken all my passions and the use I make of my senses so that, by my powerlessness, I may render You the honor which my will was unable to exact from their fury, and which I have always owed to You. I reject, with all my heart, my excessive abruptness which I renounce forevermore, whatever the temptation that may come to me from the world, the flesh, or the devil. At least, I shall do so if I am so fortunate that the Holy Spirit will deign, by the Divine Goodness, to come into my soul and to restore in it the graces with which Your goodness filled it at my Baptism. Eternal Father, I beg this mercy of You in the name of the design which You had from all eternity in the Incarnation of Your Son and through His merits. My Savior, grant me this grace for the love which you bear for the Holy Virgin. Holy Spirit, operate this marvel in Your unworthy subject by the loving union which You have from all eternity with the Father and the Son.

Subjects of meditation for the third day: Signs of having participated in the coming of the Holy Spirit.

I reflected that the Person of the Holy Spirit is in the divine essence. I saw the Spirit as the perfect bond among the three Persons in the unity of the

Trinity. I recalled the glory which the Church so frequently renders to this unity at the end of the psalms. Then, I spent a long while considering this truth: that the Godhead can be truly honored only by His own eternal glory. I saw that one of the effects of the Holy Spirit in God is union. I recalled the design of God in creating man to His image and likeness. I considered in this His three excellent faculties of which two are ordered to the third which is the will. On account of this resemblance, it seemed to me that each Person of the Blessed Trinity operated in each of these faculties, and that the Holy Spirit, by means of His unitive power, gives the will the facility to unite perfectly so that there is no disorder in the soul. This would restore it permanently to the excellence of its first state at the time of creation, making it a participant in this first glory which honors the eternal glory of God after the abundant Redemption for sin. My mind recalled the thought that I had had: that the design of the Blessed Trinity from the creation of man was that the Word should become flesh so that human nature might attain the excellence of being that God willed to give to man by the eternal union that He willed between Himself and His creature, the most admirable state of His exterior operations.

My meditation was more reflective than reasoning. I felt a great attraction for the holy humanity of Our Lord and I desired to honor and imitate it insofar as I was able in the person of the poor and of all my neighbors. I had read somewhere that He had taught us charity to make up for our powerlessness to render any service to His person. This touched my heart very particularly and very intimately.

The subject of my sixth meditation was the marks which Our Lord gives so that one may know if one has received the Holy Spirit.

The strong and tender love of Our Lord appeared clearly when He told His Apostles of the consolation that the coming of the Holy Spirit would afford them. He revealed the two forms that this consolation would take. The first was that the Holy Spirit would bear witness to Him. O my Savior, had You not given them enough by Your words and works both during Your lifetime and after Your Resurrection? What more could the Spirit of Consolation, whom the Father would send by You, do for them? O profound and inscrutable secret! O Trinity perfect in power, wisdom, and love! You bring to completion the work of founding the Holy Church. You desire her to be the Mother of all believers. To this end, You console her by instructing and strengthening her in the truths which the Incarnate Word had taught her. You infused into this Mystical Body the union of your works, giving her the power to perform miracles so as to enable her to bring to souls the true witness which You willed her to bear to Your Son. You operated in them holiness of life by the merits of the Word Incarnate. The Holy Spirit, by means of His unitive love, associates Himself to this action in order to produce the same effects by His coming. He thus renders to men the proof of the divinity and perfect manhood of Christ which should be for all a source of joy, emulation, and true detachment from worldly affections so as to form oneself according to His holy and divine actions which should lead to the resolution to live as reasonable human beings. I believe that this is what Our Lord wished to convey to His Apostles when he told them that, after the coming of the Holy Spirit, they would also bear witness to Him. This is what all Christians must do, not by bearing witness to the doctrine of Christ, which is the prerogative of apostolic men, but by the perfect actions of true Christians. Blessed are those persons who, under the guidance of Divine

Providence, are called upon to continue the ordinary practices of the life of the Son of God through the exercise of charity.

O Holy Spirit, you alone can enlighten us concerning the greatness of this mystery which, if one can say such a thing, reveals the impatience of God seen in the promptness with which he carried out His design on human nature for the perfection of the union which His omnipotence wished to operate in it. O creatures blinded by trifles, and I more than any other! Let us lift our spirits, not above what we are in the plan of God, that would be impossible, but above our natural inclinations which are due to the corruption of sin, so that in all our actions we may honor Our Lord by the witness He wishes us to bear to Him by performing the actions which he accomplished on earth and to which, on account of His love for us, He will apply the merits of His own. He wills by this means that Christians experience in this life that union with God which He has merited for us.

To this end, I shall strive, with the help of His grace, to overcome my sloth and to make use of a practice which was recommended in a reading: to look upon all the occasions for doing some good for my neighbor not only in terms of the recompense which Our Lord has promised to me because He considers such acts as done to Himself, but also in light of the fact that the neighbor has been given to me in the place of Our Lord, by means of a love which His goodness knows and which He has revealed to my heart, although I am unable to put it into words.

I shall also make use of a thought which His goodness gave me at a moment when I was distracted by a vain consideration; namely, that when I am seen accomplishing some good deed, I shall develop the habit of calling to mind the belief that God and His angels are watching me.

M.72 (On Holy Communion)

Three moments are of great importance if we wish to receive Holy Communion well. The first is the period before Communion; the second is the moment of the reception of Communion; the third is the time which follows.

During the preliminary period, we should prayerfully reflect on what Holy Communion is and who should communicate. Let us recall that faith teaches us that it is the Second Person of the Blessed Trinity in the unity of His essence. This realization should produce in us the respect that the creature owes the Creator, recognition of our dependence upon God and our own nothingness without Him, and a great desire to receive Him.

We must try to discover in God some motive for this admirable and, in a human sense, incomprehensible action. Since there is no apparent reason, other than His pure love, we must render honor and glory to God by acts of praise, adoration, love, and gratitude for His loving invention which unites Him to us. At times, we should ask Him if becoming man was not sufficient to win our hearts completely. At others, we should seek to discover what there is in us that He wanted to acquire at so high a price and offer it to Him.

The awareness of the dignity of this most Holy Sacrament should make us realize our powerlessness to prepare adequately to receive Him. Thus, we must turn to the Spirit of Love, the Holy Spirit, who furnished this gift, and beg Him to come into our hearts and to fill them with the dispositions necessary to honor the presence of such a Lord.

Sometimes, we should place before the Blessed Trinity all that the divine omnipotence has effected in us and ask the Triune God to take possession of all that is rightly His and to make use of us as He sees fit.

At other times, we should offer to God the good

202

dispositions of the Blessed Virgin and of the saints with the desire of imitating them so that we may more worthily receive Our Lord. We should do this by simple acts of our understanding and will which produce interior movements of love. However, we must preserve our souls in peace and await, with joy, the coming of Our Lord whom we must desire as the beloved of our souls.

As we reflect on those who should communicate frequently, we should humble ourselves greatly since it should be persons who are completely detached from all things, who have great love for God, and who shrink from nothing on the pathway of holy love.

The second important time for us, if we wish to communicate well, is the moment of the reception of Holy Communion. After the preceding acts have placed our souls in peace and tranquility, we must receive our God, our King, and our Spouse, in this most august sacrament. We must offer to Him acts of adoration, dependence, confidence, and abandonment of all that we are, begging Him to take possession of our being. We must unite ourselves to our Spouse to accomplish His will by means of numerous acts of love, being particularly attentive to those qualities in Him which call forth our love, especially His real presence within us. We must seek to discern what He wishes to accomplish within us, although we cannot see it.

The time following the reception of Holy Communion must be marked by a continuation of similar sentiments and acts. We must remain attentive to the divine presence and express our gratitude, sometimes to the Godhead, sometimes to each Person separately, according to His attributes. We should rejoice in contemplating this admirable invention and the loving union by which God, seeing Himself in us, makes us, once again, like unto Him. This He does, by communicating not only His grace but Himself. He thus effectively bestows upon us the merits of His life and death, thereby giving us the capacity to live in Him as He lives in us.

We can bring great simplicity to this time after the reception of Holy Communion. It is a time for thanking God by our desire to honor Him in all the actions of our lives. It is a time, also, for offering Him all the glory due to Him as God, all that He will eternally receive from the holy humanity of His Son, and all that will be rendered to Him by the blessed in heaven. This total offering can constitute an act of thanksgiving for all the benefits we have received from His divine liberality toward us.

A.61 On the Care that the Daughters of Charity Must Take to Preserve Their Company

The first reason is the eternal and inevitable misfortune due those who, on account of their malice, would cause the ruin or loss of a work which God, in His Providence, had established, as He seems to have done in the case of the Company.

The second is the loss that would be suffered by the many persons who will be called to the Company if it subsists. Should it perish, this could not be accomplished.

The third reason is the spiritual and physical harm that would befall so many poor persons were the Company to cease to exist, since they would be assisted only by the members of this Company unless God were to raise up another like it.

The fourth reason is the offense that each sister would commit against God if, through her wretched pride, she were to oppose His holy will in establishing the Company of the Daughters of Charity by doing things that would lead to the complete ruin and loss of the aforementioned Company.

II

There are many faults which the sisters might commit that could bring about the total ruin of the Company.

One of the principal offenses is to have little esteem for the manner in which the practice of the Rule calls upon the Daughters of Charity to comport themselves in all their actions.

Another is not to make known the coldness which our self-love causes us to feel for our vocation.

Another very dangerous failing is carelessness when speaking of our sisters. This could happen when the occasion presents itself to discuss what is happening in the Company, either to individuals or to the entire group, especially in matters related to the missioning of a sister who may have experienced an aversion or some repugnance for her companion. Often, it is for one who has reproved her or who desires to be very exact in fulfilling all her obligations. This could lead to criticism and blame. Sisters being sent to live with those who have been the object of such criticism are pitied. Thus, they are led to believe that the distaste that they feel for their vocation is due to the diverse dispositions of the sisters in the house where they have been placed when, in reality, it is the result of their own immortification and affection for the world as well as of the initial temptation to withdraw which they failed to reveal and concealed from their Superiors.

Since the majority of those who enter the Company are not in the habit of conversing with persons of rank, nor are they used to handling money or to possessing little things which are now freely obtainable, there is another danger which is greatly to be feared, namely, that as they become accustomed to working with the rich and the influential they may take advantage of the situation and, by forgetting the respect that they owe them, become so impudent that they are no longer bearable. Moreover, the management of money gives them the opportunity to appropriate some of it for themselves or to use it as their impulses dictate by purchasing useless objects because they have seen others with them. They might even show preferences and give some money to their relatives or others, taken not only from their resources but from the goods of the poor. Familiarity with the Ladies might lead some sisters who are already wavering and losing the affection that they should have for their vocation to obtain funds from them to give to those whom they know are ready to leave the Company.

The means for preventing the destruction of the Company on account of these dangers is to practice our Rules faithfully by observing both their general spirit and their particular recommendations, especially:

To avoid flattery and conversation with externs.

To be careful not to linger anywhere for longer than necessary.

To avoid completely conversations with men and flattery from them.

To try to return to the house early in the evening.

A.18 The Desire to Imitate Our Lord at His Death
August 16, 1658

On Monday, during the reception of Holy Communion, I suddenly felt moved by the desire that Our Lord should come to me and communicate His virtues to me. Prior to this, I seemed to experience shame for the ill-use I had made of the honor of receiving Him.

Since the subject of our morning meditation that day had been the signs which appeared at the moment of Our Savior's death, I asked Him to effect two in me. I desired firstly, that the veil of the temple, which I saw as my understanding, should be torn so that I would no longer cling to my own judgment, and secondly, that my stony heart should be rent by gentleness and support for my neighbor.

As a means for attaining this, I thought that I must turn to the example of Our Lord during the final moments of His life. Here I was instructed by His last words, "Father, into your hands I commend my spirit," which taught me that I should do nothing of consequence without this disposition. His final action was to incline His head, thereby showing me that I must not notice so many things and must humbly acquiesce to others.

M.73 On the Interior Spirit Necessary for the Daughters of Charity

It seems to me that our interior conversation with God should consist in the continuous remembrance of His holy presence. We must adore Him every hour and make acts of love for His goodness, recalling, as far as possible, the thoughts that we received during meditation so that we may correct our faults and advance in this same holy love.

On all those occasions which are painful to our senses, we must consider the paternal goodness of God. Like a good Father, He allows the rod of His divine justice to touch us, sometimes to correct us and at other times to show us His great love by allowing us to share in the sufferings of His Son so that we may likewise share in His merits. Let us, therefore, make acts of thanksgiving.

When pleasant things happen to us or when our undertakings succeed as we wish them to, before abandoning ourselves to the joy of the moment, let us glance interiorly toward God and thank Him for His mercy since it is His love alone which affords us this consolation. Therefore, let us accept it in this light by an act of love.

We must strive to use all the things that strike our senses as means to raise our minds to God. We should consider them as coming from His all-powerful hand or we should reflect on His design in creating them, which is almost always for the benefit of the human race so that it will be grateful to Him.

At other times, we should ponder the excellence of the being which God has given to us so that we may raise ourselves above the lowliness toward which our corrupted nature draws us through our affection for so many things which do not deserve to occupy our minds. Consequently, let us cry out that all that we desire on earth is God.

Sometimes we are under pressure, and it seems to us that we urgently need and hope for help from others. However, we are disappointed. This happens either through the conduct of Divine Providence or because of human weakness. We must then look immediately to the will of God and accept it in this situation. We should raise our minds to God and depend only on Him, remembering that, from all eternity, He has been and is sufficient to Himself; consequently, He can and should be sufficient for us. Since we are so fortunate as to be in a state of life in which He is to be our only consolation, we must lovingly accept the privation of all that we lack, although we consider certain things as essential for us. Let us remain in intimate peace with God without complaining of creatures who would not be a subject of trial to us if God did not permit it. We must strive to keep our minds closely united to God. Such acts must stem from our wills. Therefore, I think that it is an excellent means of keeping our minds directed toward God as is His good pleasure.

In all the situations that we have mentioned, we must develop the practice of making frequent acts of the desire to know God and ourselves. This will lead us to

make the repeated acts of love which we owe Him
and to avoid anything that is displeasing to Him. We
must often abandon ourselves to Him; show Him our
hearts filled with trust and gratitude; and try, from
time to time, to whisper ejaculatory prayers to Him.

A.27 On the Pure Love We Have Vowed to God

John 12:28-35
"Father, glorify your name!"
Then a voice came from the sky:
"I have glorified it,
and will glorify it again."
When the crowd of bystanders heard the voice, they said it was
thunder. Others maintained, "An angel was speaking to him." Jesus
answered, "That voice did not come for my sake, but for yours."
"Now has judgment come upon this world,
now will this world's prince be driven out,
and I—once I am lifted up from earth—
will draw all men to myself."
(This statement indicated the sort of death he had to die.) The crowd
objected to his words: "We have heard it said in the law that the
Messiah is to remain forever. How can you claim that the Son of Man
must be lifted up? Just who is this 'Son of Man'?"

My very dear Sisters and all souls that aspire to the
perfection of pure divine love, these are the words of
our beloved Master and Spouse who teaches us
thereby that we may hope for this and that such aspi-
rations are in keeping with His plan as seen in the
attraction that He will exert when he is raised up
from the earth.

Let us admire the means that He took to make
these words more efficacious and to enable us to
understand that they are addressed to all chosen
souls. He spoke to the entire crowd of people who
were following Him and He addressed words to His
Father in their presence that should delight us all. He
asked that His Father's name be eternally glorified by
great love.

The Father answered with a sign to show that it was, indeed, His Son who was speaking and that He had the power to fulfill His promises. The people recognized Our Lord as truly the Christ, but they asked Him who the Son of Man was since He had said that He would die and be raised up from the earth.

Was anything more needed, O my dear Spouse, so that You might be recognized? How is it that vanity prevailed and still prevails over truth? Let us be more courageous, my dear Sisters, and let us accomplish, insofar as we are able, the words God addressed to His Son when He said that His name would be glorified. May this come about through the effect of Jesus' words when He promised that He would draw all to Himself when He was lifted up. This gives dominion over all things to the Creator of all things, as is only just.

Is it not glorious for souls to cooperate with God in carrying out this plan? Let us, therefore, submit ourselves to the will of our Well-Beloved so that His words may be fulfilled in us.

What will become of us if, seeing Him raised up and desiring to draw us to Himself, we are so attached to earth that the weight of our misguided affections prevails over the attraction of His pure love?

Draw us, therefore, O my Lord, and we shall run; and the fragrance of Your perfumes will hold us so firmly that nothing will be capable of separating us from Your charity.

You desire to draw all to Yourself. Teach us truly to understand these words. If we belong to You, we can no longer belong to ourselves. If we believe that we are Yours, would it not be stealing to use ourselves and to live ever so slightly at variance with the precepts of the pure love which You taught us on earth? Once we have completely yielded our wills to the purity of Your holy love, our lives must be spent entirely in the observance of the rule given to us by our Beloved from the moment that He was lifted up until His death.

Let us take the first step in following Him which is to exclaim, "I desire it thus, my dear Spouse, I desire it thus. As proof thereof, I am going to follow You to the foot of Your Cross which I choose as my cloister. There, I shall leave behind all earthly affections because Your voice has called me and urged my heart to forget my people and my father's house so as to be open to Your great love. Therefore, at the foot of this holy, sacred, and adored Cross, I sacrifice everything that might prevent me from loving, with all the purity that You expect of me, without ever aspiring to any joy other than submission to Your good pleasure and to the laws of Your pure love."

Do not be fearful, my very dear Sisters, even if, in using the word *All,* I am making no exceptions. The thorns on these roses should not prevent you from grasping the bouquet since it will make you most pleasing to your Spouse. The Bride of the *Canticle of Canticles,* whom we should consider as our Abbess, exclaimed, "He is white and scarlet."

Since, at the creation of the world, God taught us that our resemblance to Him was dependent on His love, let us preserve this image within us by means of two eminent perfections: purity, symbolized by the color white, and charity, symbolized by the scarlet of the rose. These colors represent for us the purity and charity of God: His intrinsic purity in the simplicity of His Being and the purity inherent in all the graces that His goodness has communicated and continues to communicate with limitless generosity; the intrinsic love of God who, in the unity of His essence, engendered His Word from all eternity by His omniscience;

211

and the work of the Holy Spirit in producing Their reciprocal love, which love is the Holy Spirit. The love of God for mankind willed that the Son should take human flesh because His delight is to be among His creatures. By becoming like them, He could bear witness to the fact that God has loved them from all eternity. This He did throughout His human life upon earth.

Therefore, let us love this love and we will thereby grasp its endlessness since it depends in no way on us. Let us often recall all the actions of the life of our Beloved so that we may imitate them. Not content with the love that He bears for all chosen souls, He wishes to have some very cherished ones raised up by the purity of His love.

But, before entering upon this lofty practice, let us admire the goodness of our Spouse, and with the simplicity of the dove that He asks of us, let us question Him to discover if He loves us and if He wants us to love Him.

My Lord, I received a kind of new light concerning the uncommon love that You wish to receive from those whom You choose to exercise the purity of Your love on earth. Look upon this little flock of Yours and see if we may dare to hope for such a thing. It seems that we hold this wish in our hearts. However, the awareness of our weakness, because of our past unfaithfulness, makes us fear that You might reject us. But the thought that You placed no limits on the times that we are to forgive our enemies makes us hope that You will treat us in the same way, and so we believe that You love us.

Yes! You truly love us since You are one with the Father who willed to show us His love by giving us You, His only Son. We are also certain that You want us to love You. Both Your old and Your new law command us to do so. You promise us that Your Father will love us and that You both will come and abide with us if we love You.

O power of love! O admirable treasure hidden in the depths of the soul! O excellence of the creature who knows You! All mankind would take delight in it. Love is the gauge of a glorious eternity of souls called to heaven since, if it is alive in the soul, God will come and make His abode there.

O Pure Love, how I love You! Since You are as strong as death, separate me from all that is contrary to You.

Practice of Pure Love

My Lord, we are at the foot of the Cross where we see You hanging so that we may be drawn to You as You promised. Were not Your word omnipotent, I would fear the weight of my earthly affections. However, You are well aware of this, O my dear Savior, since You requested neither our consent nor our labor. Act resolutely in me and unite my love to Your pure love which triumphs over life.

A.31b (Thoughts on the Immaculate Conception of the Virgin Mary)

Would to God that I could fully express the thoughts that, in His goodness, He has granted to me on the subject of the Immaculate Conception of the Blessed Virgin, so that the true understanding that I possess of her merits and the desire that I have to render her fitting homage may remain always in my heart.

Thus, reflecting on this Holy Conception, I saw, at one and the same time, the design of God in the Incarnation and its application to the matter that was to form the virginal body of Mary so that, although she was a true daughter of Adam, there was to be no stain of sin in her. This was because in her was to take form the sacred body of the Son of God who could not have satisfied the divine justice by His death had He participated in original sin. The most pure body of the Blessed Virgin is a worthy dwelling place for the soul that God created for her. Both are agreeable to God because, from the moment of her pure Conception, both have been enriched by the merits of the death of her Son.

As into a very precious vessel, more and more graces have been poured into her soul and she has never failed to make good use of them. Therefore, with every good reason, she should be honored by all creatures and served in a particular way by Christians since she is the only pure creature who has always found grace in the eyes of God. This makes her the astonishment of the heavenly court and the admiration of all humanity.

The Immaculate Conception of the Blessed Virgin leads us to realize and to adore the omnipotence of God because grace totally vanquished nature in her. She was saved without ever having been lost, not only through mercy but also through justice, since this was essential for the Incarnation of the Son of God in the eternal plan for the Redemption of mankind. We must, therefore, honor this holy Conception that made her so precious in the eyes of God, and believe that it depends only on us to receive the assistance of the Blessed Virgin in all our needs. This is so because it seems to me that it would be impossible for God to refuse her anything. His divine and loving glance never left her since she always lived according to His will. Therefore, we must be convinced that He is always ready to grant whatever she requests because she asks for nothing that is not for His glory and our good.

We must carefully consider the advantages that the

Blessed Virgin has enjoyed over all other creatures as a consequence of her Immaculate Conception. The first is that she never harbored tendencies that could push her to sin. She never knew this evil that dwells in all the children of Adam. Oh, what peace, gentleness, charity, and humility there was in the soul of the Virgin since it is this instinct that causes us so much trouble by leading us into sin.

The knowledge that God gives us of the Immaculate Conception of the Blessed Virgin should cause us to glorify Him eternally for this masterpiece of His omnipotence in a nature that is purely human. We are also led to admire the beauty of the purity of Our Lady's thoughts. Her mind never indulged in useless thoughts nor was it occupied with sin.

May the frailty of human beings, conceived in sin that leads them to revolt against God, bring to light the honor that the Blessed Virgin rendered to Him by remaining immersed in justice and truth. May souls devoted to the holy and most pure Virgin attentively consider her actions which were never in the least disagreeable to God since they were always accomplished according to His will.

The Immaculate Conception of the Blessed Virgin, therefore, completely enlightened her mind and strengthened her will so that she continually acted in such a way that she never omitted anything that God asked of her. Consequently, she was filled with virtue both in the matter and in the form of the being which God gave to her.

This is why, throughout my life, in time and in eternity, I desire to love and to honor her to the best of my ability by my gratitude to the Blessed Trinity for the choice made of the Holy Virgin to be so closely united to the Divinity. I wish to honor the three Persons separately and also together in the unity of the divine essence.

M.5b (The Virgin Mary, Co-redemptrix)

(August 1659)

On August 15, 1659,[50] during the Holy Sacrifice of the Mass at which I was to receive Holy Communion, I reflected on the greatness of the Blessed Virgin as Mother of the Son of God who desired to honor her to such a degree that we may say that she participated in some way in all the mysteries of His life and that she contributed to His humanity by her virginal blood and milk. Considering her in this light, I congratulated Mary on her excellent dignity which unites her to her Son in the perpetual sacrifice of the Cross, reenacted and offered on our altars.

I also remarked that, by this means, the Son of God has, as it were, begotten human nature for Eternity, rendering it capable of enjoying God according to His designs. This appeared to me to be great in heaven where the just contemplate the divine nature and essence; angelic nature; and human nature which, in turn, is also contemplated by the angels and the divinized humanity of Our Lord.

A.100 (Problems for the Company)

(1660)[51]

The method of teaching used at La Fère is to be feared not only because the sister involved may inject much of herself into it and advance maxims that she cannot explain, but also because public places, such as the rooms in hospitals where the Blessed Sacrament is kept, are used. This could lead others to accuse the Superiors of the Daughters of Charity of allowing the sisters to undertake too much.

There are also other disadvantages. God was pleased to choose village girls for the solid establishment of the Servants of the Sick Poor. Now, since this method of instruction is brilliant and sophisticated, if those sisters who have great capabilities were permitted to

216

undertake it but were not dispensed from more lowly tasks, they might, after having been well trained for it, seek dispensations from several exercises and expect better treatment than that given to those in more humble duties. If contradicted in this matter, they would soon leave the Company.

Other sisters would turn to avid reading. In the desire to appear capable, they would devote their attention to learning without taking into consideration other necessary work. Although they have recently arrived in the Company, they would not apply themselves to the practice of mortification. There are already examples of this truth in the Company.

It is said that this work will not continue for a long period of time; that there will not always be sisters capable of undertaking it; that it has the approval of the Pastor and of the Vicar General; and that most of the inhabitants of the city applaud it. This would be acceptable for individuals such as Mademoiselle Pileure or for others whom God might wish to assemble for this purpose.

However, to turn this into an essential function in the Company of the Daughters of Charity would be to enter on the pathway to its destruction. At the very least, it would divide it into two bodies. Those who would judge themselves capable of this employment would be the dominant group and, in their illusions of grandeur, they would fulfill the functions of Saint Mary Magdalen. They would compromise and they would lord it over those employed in visiting the sick. Little by little, poor girls would be prevented from entering the Company and the others would soon become ladies. This is already the pretense of several sisters.

It could be objected that one of the main functions of the establishment of the Confraternity and the

Company of the Daughters of Charity is the spiritual service of the sick poor. We are all convinced of the truth of this. May God be glorified for it! But does not the grace of God act in all the sisters even the most rustic and simple? In the places where they are located, how many people have been turned away from sin? How many general confessions have been made after years away from this sacrament? How many little girls have been instructed by the sisters in the school? How many persons in the families to which she brings food have also profited from her instruction? How many heretics have been converted since the Daughters of Charity have been working in the hospitals? Recall that, in 1659, a sister who had been in the hospital of Saint-Denis said that, during the year, five or six heretics were converted, including the son of a Protestant minister, without counting several previous conversions. All this was done under a veil of silence. Would to God that it had not been necessary to mention it, since this manner of acting is in keeping with the first commandments of the Founder of the Company, Jesus Christ, speaking through His servant. We are told to honor His Hidden Life. This is essential for the strength of this Company which, one day, may perhaps have the grace to be employed, not in the city, but in the service of the peasants according to its original end or, rather, according to God's first design for it. This could come about in the course of changes inherent in human history.

O what a happiness, if, without offending God, the Company could be employed only in the service of those who are destitute in all things! To this end, this Company must never depart from nor change its poor manner of life. Thus, should Divine Providence provide them with more than is necessary, let them go to serve the corporally and spiritually poor at their own expense. If this passes unnoticed, what does it matter, so long as souls honor eternally the Redemption of Our Lord?

M.8b   (On Holy Communion)

On the Feast of Saint Genevieve, in 1660, as I was receiving Holy Communion, I felt, upon seeing the Sacred Host, an extraordinary thirst which had its origin in the belief that Jesus wanted to give Himself to me in the simplicity of His divine infancy. When I was receiving Him and for a long time afterward, my mind was filled by an interior communication which led me to understand that Jesus was bringing not only Himself to me but also all the merits of His mysteries. This communication lasted all day. It was not a forced, interior preoccupation. It was rather a presence or a recurrent recollection, as sometimes happens when something is troubling me.

I felt that I was being warned that, since Jesus had given Himself entirely to me, laden with the merits of all these mysteries, I must make use of this occasion to participate in His submission to humiliations.

One means to attain this end is to be found in the fact that, without any cause in me, I appear to others as having received some graces from God. This both humbles me and gives me courage.

No desires, no resolutions. The grace of my God will accomplish in me whatever He wills.

A.49   Prayer Before Holy Communion

Most Holy Spirit, the Love of the Father and of the Son, come to purify and to embellish my soul so that it will be agreeable to my Savior and so that I may receive Him for His greater glory and my salvation. I long for You with all my heart, O Bread of Angels. Do not consider my unworthiness which keeps me away from You, but listen only to Your love that has so often invited me to approach You. Give Yourself entirely to me, my God. May Your precious body, Your holy soul, and Your glorious divinity, which I adore in this Holy Sacrament, take complete possession of me.

Sweet Jesus! Gentle Jesus! My God and my All! Have mercy on all souls redeemed by Your precious blood. Inflame them with the arrow of Your love in order to make them grateful for the love that urged You to give Yourself to us in the Blessed Sacrament.

To this end, I offer You the glory that You enjoy within Yourself from all eternity, and all the graces that You granted the Blessed Virgin and the saints, together with the glory that they will eternally render You by this same love.

SPIRITUAL TESTAMENT

My dear Sisters, I continue to ask God for His blessings for you and pray that He will grant you the grace to persevere in your vocation in order to serve Him in the manner He asks of you.

Take good care of the service of the poor. Above all, live together in great union and cordiality, loving one another in imitation of the union and life of Our Lord.

Pray earnestly to the Blessed Virgin, that she may be your only Mother.[52]

NOTES

[1] Louise de Marillac (Aug. 12, 1591-Mar. 15, 1660) had wanted to be a Capuchin Nun. She had undoubtedly made a promise to God to do so. However, Father Champigny, her first spiritual director, told her that her delicate health would not permit her to become a religious. Following the advice of her family, Louise married Antoine LeGras on February 5, 1613. He was secretary to the Queen Marie de Medicis. Their son, Michel, was born the following October 18.

[2] Pierre Camus, Bishop of Belley, a friend of the de Marillacs and of Francis de Sales.

[3] Sunday, June 4, 1623.

[4] The Church of Saint-Nicolas-des-Champs, rue Saint-Martin, the parish church of Louise de Marillac.

[5] Vincent de Paul was, at the time, a tutor in the de Gondi household which was situated in the Parish of Saint-Sauveur.

[6] Francis de Sales, Bishop of Geneva and Founder of the Visitation, had died in Dec. 1622.

[7] After 1628, the Priests of the Mission were known as the Congregation of the Mission.

[8] See *Coste* I. 51

[9] *The Treatise on the Love of God* by Francis de Sales.

[10] Letter from M. Vincent to Louise de Marillac *(Coste* I. 75).

[11] Antoine Legras and Louise de Marillac were married on February 5, 1613.

[12] See the Letter of M. Vincent *(Coste* I, 156).

[13] See the Letter of M. Vincent *(Coste* I. 181).

[14] See the Letter of M. Vincent *(Coste* I. 200).

[15] These notes seemed to have been used in drawing up report no. 52, of which they faithfully give nearly all the details.

[16] M. Vincent asked her to make these visitations after the death of Marguerite Naseau *(Coste* I. 188).

[17] Draft drawn up before the Rule of 1645 *(Coste* XIII. 551).

[18] Correction by Vincent de Paul.

[19] Correction by Vincent de Paul.

[20] Louise de Marillac originally wrote "establishments," but she crossed it out and wrote "foundation."

[21] These thoughts, drawn up on different days, are contained in the same small notebook as A. 21.

[22] The French text uses "adorez." This shows the influence of her study of Latin. She uses it, as it is used in Sacred Scripture, to mean "prostrate yourself."

[23] See the Letter of M. Vincent *(Coste* II, 114).

[24] After the Motherhouse of the Daughters of Charity was moved to the Saint-Denis district, near Saint-Lazare.

[25] The Rules on which Louise de Marillac makes her observations were possibly drawn up after the Conference of June 14, 1643 *(Leonard* 102).

²⁶ A. 90 comes after the passage on the Hotel-Dieu.

²⁷ A. 90 carries the Roman numeral II. It comes in the middle of A. 91.

²⁸ Because of a large tear in the manuscript of this passage, the lines are incomplete. However, they have been completed through reference to corresponding passages from the copy of the Rule of Angers, evidently written by Louise de Marillac.

²⁹ Correction by Vincent de Paul.

³⁰ Note made by Vincent de Paul: "Either the chaplain or the Sister Servant shall keep the register of the admission and release of the sick."

³¹ Correction by Vincent de Paul.

³² Note made by Vincent de Paul: "If it is the responsibility of the Sister Servant to keep the register."

³³ These topics proposed by Louise de Marillace were treated by Vincent de Paul in a series of Conferences in 1646 (*Leonard* 214; 226; 232; 249).

³⁴ Marie Despinal died in May, 1646.

³⁵ The accident occurred in June, 1642, on the vigil of the Feast of Pentecost.

³⁶ Thoughts drawn up by Louise de Marillac for the Conference (*Leonard* 304).

³⁷ Louise de Marillac used to prepare her thoughts in writing on the subject of the Conference being given by Vincent de Paul. At the beginning of the Company, it was she who drew up the account of the Conference from Vincent de Paul's notes, from the sisters' letters, and from whatever the sisters remembered. In May 1646, she confides this duty to her secretary, Sister Elizabeth Hellot, who will be replaced in 1652 by Julienne Loret, and then by Mathurine Guérin. The secretaries saved many of the letters of their Foundress.

³⁸ Thoughts prepared in view of the Conference (*Leonard* 468).

³⁹ This vow formula is signed by Jeanne Delacroix who recopied it as far as the word "chastity." The rest is written by Louise de Marillac.

⁴⁰ The date is mentioned on the copy made by Marguerite Chétif.

⁴¹ Probably the house at Saint-Denis where Sister Claude Brigide was assigned in 1652.

⁴² See Letter 76b, *Letters.*

⁴³ Thoughts prepared for the Conference (*Leonard* 615). Louise de Marillace had read only the first part when Vincent de Paul stopped her to give an explanation.

⁴⁴ Thoughts prepared for the Conference (*Leonard* 687).

⁴⁵ Thoughts prepared for the Conference (*Leonard* 697).

⁴⁶ Henriette Gesseaume, Marie-Marthe Trumeau, and Renée Delacroix.

⁴⁷ Jeanne Gressier.

⁴⁸ The difficulties are going to increase in 1657 (Letter 535, *Letters*).

⁴⁹ Thoughts prepared for a Conference, possibly that of June 6, 1656 on Indifference (*Leonard* 767).

⁵⁰ The person copying this passage had written "1660." This date is impossible since Louise de Marillac had died Mar. 15, 1660.

[51] See Letter 650, *Letters.*

[52] This Spiritual Testament was recorded by the sisters who attended Louise de Marillac during her final moments on earth. It was faithfully transcribed. Gobillon quotes it in his *Life of Mademoiselle LeGras,* written in 1676.

NUMERICAL LISTING OF WRITINGS

226

228

CONVERSION TABLE
English and French Editions

Eng.	Fr.	Eng.	Fr.	Eng.	Fr.
3	3	35	707, 708	67	725, 726
4	3, 687	36	708	68	726
5	687, 688	37	708, 709	69	726, 727
6	688	38	709	70	727, 728
7	688, 689	39	709, 710	71	728
8	689, 690	40	710, 711	72	728, 729
9	690	41	711	73	729, 730
10	690, 691	42	711, 712	74	730
11	691, 692	43	712, 713	75	730, 731
12	692	44	713	76	731, 732
13	692, 693	45	713, 714	77	732, 733
14	693, 694	46	714	78	733
15	694	47	715	79	733, 734
16	694, 695	48	715, 716	80	734
17	695, 696	49	716	81	734, 735
18	696	50	716, 717	82	735, 736
19	696, 697	51	717, 718	83	736
20	697, 698	52	718	84	736, 737
21	698	53	718, 719	85	737
22	698, 699	54	719, 720	86	737, 738
23	699, 700	55	720	87	738, 739
24	700	56	720, 721	88	739
25	700, 701	57	721	89	739, 740
26	701, 702	58	blank	90	740, 741
27	702	59	chapter title	91	741
28	702, 703	60	blank	92	741, 742
29	703, 704	61	722	93	742
30	704	62	722, 723	94	742, 743
31	704, 705	63	723, 724	95	743, 744
32	705, 706	64	724	96	744
33	706	65	724, 725	97	745
34	706, 707	66	725	98	745, 746

Eng.	Fr.	Eng.	Fr.	Eng.	Fr.
99	746	133	765, 766	167	788, 789
100	746, 747	134	766	168	789, 790
101	747, 748	135	767	169	790
102	748	136	767, 768	170	790, 791
103	748, 749	137	768, 769	171	791, 792
104	749	138	769	172	792
105	750	139	769, 770	173	792, 793
106	750, 751	140	770	174	793, 794
107	751	141	770, 771	175	794
108	751, 752	142	771, 772	176	794, 795
109	752	143	772, 773	177	795, 796
110	752, 753	144	773	178	796
111	753, 754	145	773, 774	179	796, 797
112	754	146	774, 775	180	797
113	754, 755	147	775	181	797, 798
114	755	148	775, 776	182	798
115	755, 756	149	776, 777	183	799
116	756	150	777	184	799, 800
117	757	151	777, 778	185	800
118	757, 758	152	778, 779	186	800, 801
119	758	153	779	187	801
120	758, 759	154	779, 780	188	802
121	759, 760	155	780, 781	189	802, 803
122	760, 761	156	781	190	803
123	761	157	781, 782	191	803, 804
124	761, 762	158	782	192	804, 805
125	762	159	782, 783	193	805
126	blank	160	783, 784	194	805, 806
127	chapter title	161	784	195	806, 807
128	blank	162	785	196	807
129	763	163	785, 786	197	807, 808
130	763, 764	164	786, 787	198	808
131	764, 765	165	787, 788	199	808, 809
132	765	166	788	200	809, 810

Eng.	Fr.	Eng.	Fr.	Eng.	Fr.
201	810	208	814, 815	215	819
202	810, 811	209	815, 816	216	819, 820
203	811	210	816	217	820, 821
204	812	211	816, 817	218	821
205	812, 813	212	817	219	821, 822
206	813, 814	213	817, 818	220	822
207	814	214	818, 819	221	823

INDEX

ABANDONMENT to God: 8, 10, 15, 17, 22, 44, 203. see also: Divine Providence.

ABASEMENT of God: 40. see also: Humility, Incarnation.

ABSOLUTION: 194.

ACCIDENT at the Motherhouse: see Fall.

ACCORD: 103, 133, 134.

ACCOUNTS see Bookkeeping. —giving accounts: 106, 107, 135.

ACCUSATIONS of the sisters —accepting them: 132.

ACT of Faith, Hope and Charity: 97, 134. —of Contrition: 134. —of Adoration, see Adoration.

ADAM —his sin: 140, 171.

ADHERENCE to Jesus Christ: 152. see Obedience and also Abandonment, Love.

ADMISSION to the Company. —of poor girls: 217.

ADORATION: 78, 92, 129, 130, 202. see also: Blessed Sacrament.

AFFECTION —toward the sick: see Charity, Cordiality, Service of the poor.

AFFLICTED, The —consoling them: see the Poor.

ALLOWANCES paid to the sisters: 135. —unpaid: 164.

ALMS —their purpose: 75. —for the poor of the Confraternities: 50, 53, 67.

ANGEL: 69, 75, 201, 216. —guardian angel: 45, 70, 110, 130. —devotion to the guardian angel: 7, 134, 140. —of Louise de Marillac: 12.

ANGELUS: 77, 174.

ANTOINE, Brother: 94.

APOSTLES —awaiting the Holy Spirit: 26, 43, 44, 124, 173, 174, 196, 200. —the preaching of the Gospel: 8. —the washing of the feet: 48. —devotion to: 7.

ARGUING of the sisters with the galley slaves: 83.

ASCENSION: 13, 26, 173, 196. —and Mary: 193. —time from the Ascension to Pentecost: 124. see also: Apostles.

ASNIÈRES —visit of the Confraternity by Louise de Marillac: 27.

ASSISTANT —her duties: 77, 80, 88, 104, 187.

ASSUMPTION of Mary: 14.

ATTENTION to the needs of the sick: 92, 93, 184, 185. see Needs —of Louise de Marillac to the person of each sister: 115, 116, 181, 182.

AUTHORITY —how to utilize it: 145, 192.

AVAILABILITY to the Holy Spirit: 10, 11, 73, 196. —with regard to placement and apostolic assignments: 63, 64, 65, 155.

BAKER —her duties: 116.

BAPTISM: 11, 151, 196, 198. —of foundlings: 79. —of Our Lord: 47.

BEDDING for the sick: 52, 56.

BEDS of the sick —making them: 83, 90.

BELL at the Motherhouse: 77, 110, 178.

BELL-RINGER —her duties: 110, 178.

BIRTH of Louise de Marillac: 35.

BLESSED SACRAMENT —adoration: 68, 69, 70, 120. —visit: 68. —presence in the hospital rooms: 216.

BLOOD of Jesus Christ: 175, 176.

BLOODLETTING: 86, 116.

BODY —created by God: 139, 171. —its needs: 171. —taking care of it: 176.

BOOKKEEPING: 64, 106, 116. —keeping an exact account: 84, 116. —separating the accounts of the poor from those of the Community: 135.

BORROWING of money: 164.

BOUILLON for the sick: 32, 90, 91, 95, 96, 182.

BREAD: 69, 116. —bread oven: 67. —for the foundlings: 76. —for the sick: 32.

BULLES —visit of the Confraternity by Louise de Marillac: 51, 55.

BURIAL of members of the Confraternities: 29, 50, 53.

CALL of God —vocation is a call: 122, 124, 137, 159, 204.

CARE of the mouths of the sick: 95. —of sick sisters: 182, 184. —of the sick: see the Sick.

CATECHISM: 69, 86, 113, 114, 216. —teach it with simplicity: 216. —to children: 76. —to young people: 86, 113. —among the sisters: 62, 79.

CHANGE in placement of the sisters —after long reflection: 78. —to welcome a sister at the time she is changed: 191. —not to criticize the sisters: 205. —thoughts of Louise de Marillac on the necessity of change: 190.

CHANTILLY —financial difficulties: 164.

CHARITY: 34. —of Jesus Christ: 12, 31, 46. see also Love, God, Jesus Christ. —spirit of the Daughters of Charity: 162. —living it: 200, 201. —toward the poor: 20, 22, 119. —toward everyone: 177. —among the sisters: 64, 109, 177, 182, 221. —requiring the defense of persons not present: 177. see also Cordiality, Respect, Forbearance.

234

—among the members of the Confraternities: 32, 49-56. see also: Confraternities.

CHASTITY —the vow: 75. —see Prudence in comportment.

CHÂTEAUDUN: 170.

CHRISTIAN WOMAN —to live as a good one: 6, 57, 108, 140, 150, 177, 200, 201.

CHRISTMAS: 24. see also: Crib, Nativity.

CHURCH, The: 56, 70, 73, 199, 200; militant: 10, 172; suffering: 172; triumphant: 172. —and the devotion to Mary: 150, 151. —and Louise de Marillac: 74. —Daughters of Charity, daughters of the Church: 5. —Priests of the Mission in the service of the Church: 15. —upkeep of the churches: 87.

CLEANLINESS —of the cook: 118. —in the hospital: 93.

CLERGY: 57. see also: Congregation of the Mission.

COLLECTION taken up by the Confraternities of Charity: 29, 51.

COMMUNICATION —with Superiors: 169. —with the world: 136. —necessary between the Assistant and the Superioress: 104-106.

COMMUNION: 16, 69, 79, 142, 219. see also: Eucharist. —meditations of Louise de Marillac: 37, 124, 141, 202, 219. —com-

munions of Louise de Marillac: 8, 71, 206. —taken to homes: 50, 66. —First Communion of the children: 114. —of the sick: 89. see also Sacraments. —prayer of Louise de Marillac: 219.

COMMUNITY —joined together by the love of God: see Charity, Union. —joined together for the service of the poor: 130. see also: Community Life, Sharing.

COMMUNITY LIFE: 86, 175. —fraternity: see Cordiality, Gentleness, Respect, Forebearance, Union. —in the image of the Blessed Trinity: see Trinity, Union. —its difficulties: see Discord. —regarding the service of the poor: 131, 154. —poor, simple life: see Simplicity. —life of sharing: see Community sharing, Goods.

COMMUNITY SHARING: 123, 130, 133, 175. —of goods: 186. —with the poor: 109.

COMPANY of the Daughters of Charity —led and willed by God: 153, 165, 204, 217. —dependent upon the Church: 74. —made up of village girls: 63, 216. see also: Origins. —and of widows: 63. —its end: 123, 165, 204, 217. see also: Service of the poor. —its spirit: 162, 166. —confidence in Divine Providence: 129. —graces which God has bestowed upon it: 124. —its strengthening: 122. —its future: 154, 165, 204, 216. —the sisters must love it: 121. —Mary, the only Mother: 74, 221.

COMPASSION toward the poor: 82, 134, 184.

COMPLAINTS against the sisters, see Accusations. —of the sisters against the Company: 205.

CONFERENCES to the Daughters of Charity —of Monsieur Vincent: Louise de Marillac requests them: 120. —of Louise de Marillac: 77, 78. —on the deceased sisters: 121. —among sisters: 123. —to the Ladies of Charity: see Meetings. —Friday conferences: 79, 123.

CONFESSION —dispositions: 44. —thoughts of Louise de Marillac: 194. —extraordinary confessions of the sick: 90, 97, 98.

CONFESSOR —chosen by Superiors: 134. —one only for the Community: 134. —respect for: see Respect.

CONFLANS —visit of the Confraternity by Louise de Marillac: 29.

CONFRATERNITY OF CHARITY —organization: 28, 156. —and the Congregation of the Mission: 156. —Asnières: 27. —Bulles: 51, 55. —St.-Cloud: 27. —Gournay: 50, 54, 65. —Hôtel-Dieu: 157. —Neufville-Roy: 51, 54. —Pont-Sainte-Maxence: 50, 53. —Verneuil: 49, 52. —Confraternity, name of the Company of the Daughters of Charity: 63.

CONGREGATION OF THE MISSION —work of God: 16. —its end, its spirit: 15, 16. —spiritual assistance to the sisters: 119. see also: Visit. —responsibility with regard to the Confraternities: 156.

CONVERSION: 11, 12, 25. —prayer for: 74, 200. —of sinners: 21.

COOK of the Motherhouse: 117. —her duties: 181.

CORDIALITY: 86, 132, 155, 176, 184, 191, 221. —toward the Sister Servant: 176. —of the Superioress toward the sisters: 103, 104. —toward everyone: 123, 131, 133.

CORRESPONDENCE: see Letters.

COUNCIL of the Company: 170.

CRAFTSMEN: 163, 164.

CREATION: 17, 33, 73, 144, 148, 171, 173, 195, 199, 207. —new creation: 73.

CRIB —the mystery: 10, 46. see also: Nativity.

CROSS of Christ: 35, 211, 216. —meditation of Louise de Marillac: 137.

CURIOSITY: 113, 116, 167, 180, 205.

DAILY OFFERING —prayer of Louise de Marillac: 125.

DARKNESS of soul: 35.

DAUGHTER OF CHARITY —her vocation: 155. —servant of the poor: 181. see also: Service of the poor, Vocation. —her virtues, her spirit: see Charity, Humility, Simplicity, Spirit.

DEATH —of Jesus Christ: 13, 18, 23, 98, 151, 206. —of Mary: 14. —reflection on death: 44, 151. —see also: Preparation for death. —death to self: see Mortification.

DEFENSE —defending sisters who are not present: 177.

DELACROIX, Jeanne D.C. —formula of the vows: 146.

DELACROIX, Renée D.C. —Paris: 170.

DESPINAL, Marie D.C. —conference on her virtues: 121.

DETACHMENT: 196, 197.

DEVIL: 43, 45.

DEVOTION toward the Virgin Mary: 150. see also: Angelus, Mary, Rosary.

DIRECTRESS of the Seminary —her duties: 107.

DISCERNMENT —vocation of new arrivals: 108. —necessary for proper conduct: 105, 130.

DISCORD among the sisters: 153, 154. —among the members of the Confraternities: 51, 55.

DISCRETION —among the sisters: 87, 114, 116, 132, 170, 204. —toward persons not belonging to the Community: 155. —of the Superioress: 102-104. —in certain duties: 111, 114, 116, 180. —of the Company over the good accomplished: 217.

DIVINE LAW: 136, 212.

DIVINE PROVIDENCE: 12. —abandonment to: 73, 133. —trust in: 71. —submission to: 43, 123. —its direction of the Company: 122. —source of all graces: 141. —direction of the life of Louise de Marillac: 41.

DREAM of Louise de Marillac: 73.

DRUGEON, Madeleine D.C. —in Poland: 159.

DYING, The: 15, 18.

EASTER: 70. —meditation of Louise de Marillac: 49.

EDIFICATION of one's neighbor: see Witness.

EDUCATION of the sisters by Louise de Marillac: see Attention to the person, Warnings, the Poor, Prayer, Community Life. —of the children: see School, Schoolgirls.

ELDERLY: see Hospice.

ELECTION of Officers: 66.

EMPLOYMENT of the Daughter of Charity: see Vocation. —lowly employment: 216.

ENEMIES —love them: 20.

EPIPHANY: 75.

EQUALITY among the sisters: 175, 182.

237

ESPOUSAL of Louise de Marillac: see Marriage. —spiritual: 27.

ESTABLISHMENT —difficulties at the beginning: 131.

ESTEEM —for one's neighbor: 160. —for one's sisters: 120. —thoughts of Louise de Marillac: 152. see also: Cordiality, Gentleness, Respect, Forbearance. —for one's vocation: see Vocation.

EUCHARIST: 16, 37, 202. —and the Trinity: 202. —and the Incarnation: 148, 202. —and the Redemption: 214. —and the Holy Spirit: 202. —adoration: 69, 70. —actual presence in the house: 203, 216. see also: Communion, Blessed Sacrament.

EVANGILIZATION: see Spiritual Service, Catechism.

EXAMINATION —of conscience; particular: 61, 62; general: 6, 62, 92. —of Louise de Marillac: 147.

EXPENDITURES —for the galley slaves: 83. see also: Bookkeeping, Money.

EXTREME UNCTION: 90.

FAITH: see God, Jesus Christ, Incarnation, Redemption, Trinity. —living in faith: 27, 64. —cultivating it in the poor: 134. see also: Spiritual Service.

FALL of the ceiling: 122.

FASTING: 7, 75.

FAULTS —of the sisters: 88. see also: Accusations. —conduct to be maintained by the Sister Servant: 88. see also: Warnings. —accepting warnings: see Spiritual Charity. —faults of the older girls: see Punishment.

FEARS of Louise de Marillac for the Company: 154, 204, 216.

FEEDING of the sick: 90, 95. see also: Food.

FEVER —caring for those with a fever: 86.

FIACRE, St. —meditation of Louise de Marillac: 138.

FIDELITY to God: 10, 123.

FLIGHT into Egypt: 39.

FOOD —of the sick: 93. see also: Regulations of the hospitals. —of the sisters; do not eat the food of the poor: see Life Style, Moderation, Cook, Portress.

FORBEARANCE —virtue of the Daughters of Charity. —among sisters: 86, 103, 119, 155, 167. —toward everyone: 123. —in imitation of Jesus Christ: 150. see also: Imitation of Jesus Christ.

FORGIVENESS of Jesus Christ: 23. —requesting forgiveness: see Request for Forgiveness.

FORMATION of the sisters: 61-65, 107-110, 112-114, 122. —goal of the formation: 154, 216. —professional formation: 116.

FOUNDLINGS — their instruction: see School, Schoolgirls. — Rule for the Daughters of Charity in their service: 75, 80, 188.

FRANCE — pray for it: 57.

FRANCIS DE SALES, St. — Treatise on the Love of God: 26.

FRANCONVILLE — visit of the Confraternity by Louise de Marillac: 29.

FRATERNAL SHARING: 118, 153. — for the service of the poor: 130.

FREE WILL of man: 195.

FREEDOM of man: 149, 171, 195.

FRIENDSHIP among the sisters: 144.

GALLEY SLAVES — Rule for the sisters in their service: 83.

GAZE of Jesus: 141. — of faith on the poor: see the Poor, Service of the Poor.

GENEVIÈVE, D.C. — Châteaudun: 170. — Paris: 170.

GENTLENESS: 4. — toward the poor: 20, 22, 82, 134. — among the sisters: 119, 155. — toward everyone: 93, 123, 134. — of the Sister Servant toward her companions: 103, 106. — in actions and words: 106, 182. — in imitation of Jesus Christ: 22, 150. — in imitation of Mary: 214.

GESSEAUME, Henriette D.C.: 170.

GIFT OF SELF TO GOD: 162, 195. — in order to serve one's neighbor: 47. see also: Service of God. — of Louise de Marillac: 9, 24, 26, 44.

GIFTS — not to be accepted from the schoolgirls: 114.

GIFTS OF THE HOLY SPIRIT: 196.

GIRLS — poor little girls: see School, Schoolgirls.

GLORY OF GOD: 14, 17, 43, 133, 199.

GOD — meditation of Louise de Marillac: 11, 15, 171, 174, 202, 207. — Creator: 17, 20, 195, 207. — charity of: 11, 34, 171, 207. — relationship of the soul to: 202. — presence in the poor: 199, 218. see also: the Poor. — teaching about God: see Spiritual Service. — God: see Abandonment, Glory, Goodness, Humility, Love, Mercy, Divine Providence, Will of God, Wisdom. — His perfection: 21, 42.

GOODNESS — of God: 21, 25. — toward one's neighbor: 19.

GOODS — of the poor: 50, 53, 67, 100, 206. — of the Community; placed in common: 186. — of the Confraternities: see Confraternities.

GOSPEL — reading: 4, 62. — preached by the Apostles: 8.

GOURNAY — visit of the Confraternity by Louise de Marillac: 50, 54, 65.

239

GOURNAY, Mme. de: 66.

GOVERNMENT of the Company: see Superioress General, Officers, Sister Servant, Authority, Accord.

GRACE of God: 39, 171, 196, 197.

GRESSIER, Jeanne D.C. —Suggested for duty in Châteaudun: 171.

HAIR SHIRT: 7.

HARDEMONT, Anne D.C. —Montreuil-sur-Mer: 129.

HEALTH —a precious treasure: 185. —of the children: 188. —of Louise de Marillac: see Illness. —of the sisters: see Sisters.

HEART of Mary: 14.

HELL: 20. see also: Devil.

HERBLAY —visit of the Confraternity by Louise de Marillac: 29.

HERETIC —conversion of: 218.

HIDDEN LIFE of Jesus Christ. —in Mary's womb: 71. —in Nazareth: 40, 47, 218.

HOLY SPIRIT: 7, 73, 123, 124, 170, 200. —and the Church: 7, 73. —and the Apostles: 26. —and Mary: 14. —dispositions necessary for His reception: 44, 173, 195-201. —novena, prayer: 4, 84, 112. —meditations of Louise de Marillac: 26, 173, 195. —prayers of Louise de Marillac: 196, 197, 219. —The Congregation of the Mission is His creation: 16. —see also: Pentecost.

HOLY WATER: 75, 93.

HOPE in God: 6, 11.

HOSPICE of the Name of Jesus. —Organization: 162. —work of those housed there: 163.

HOSPITAL —Rule: 88, 89, 95. —Service of the sick: 89, 95, 96. —Hospital: see also: Le Mans, Saint-Denis.

HÔTEL-DIEU —Rule for the Daughters of Charity: 81.

HUMAN NATURE: 135, 195, 208, 216. see also: Man.

HUMANITY of Jesus Christ: 19, 25, 26, 41, 46, 70, 143, 149, 174, 199, 204, 216.

HUMILITY: 4, 20, 118, 132, 148, 154, 160. —in the service of the poor: 82. —requesting it of God: 40, 203. —and the Company of the Daughters of Charity: 162, 218. —in imitation of Jesus Christ: 22, 24, 150. —humility of God: 12, 20, 21, 22, 24, 47. —of Mary: 13, 47, 136, 150, 193, 214. —of Louise de Marillac: 145, 167. —of the Officers: 103.

HUMOR of Louise de Marillac: 179.

HUNGER —need: 72. —for justice: 72.

HYGIENE in the hospital: 90, 93.

ICAR, Monsieur: 84.

IGNORANCE —damaging in the service of the poor: 154.

ILLNESS —how to bear with it: 82. —of the sisters: see Sisters. —of Louise de Marillac: 191.

IMITATION of Jesus Christ: 12, 25, 40, 47, 177, 199, 221. —of His pilgrimage on earth: 139. —of His charity for the poor: 62. —in His bearing with accusations: 183. —of Jesus Crucified: 70. —of Mary: 14, 26.

IMMACULATE CONCEPTION: 13, 71, 73, 193, 213.

IMPATIENCE —overcoming it: 22.

INCARNATION: 5, 10, 15, 20, 24, 38, 70, 71, 74, 75, 136, 142, 149, 172, 195, 198, 200, 212, 216. —and the Eucharist: 148-150. —meditation of Louise de Marillac: 171, 200.

INDIFFERENCE: see Availability.

INFIDELITY to the Rule, ruin of the Company: 165. see also: Rule.

INFIRMARIAN —her duties at the Motherhouse: 184.

INTERIOR TRIALS of Louise de Marillac: 8, 9, 146.

JESUS CHRIST —in Mary's womb: 71. —Nativity: 24, 46, 135. see also: Humanity, Incarnation, Nativity, Christmas. —life in Nazareth: 40, 47. —baptism: 47. —in the desert: 43. —pilgrim: 139. —suffering: 10. —death on the Cross: 8, 11. see also Paschal Mystery, Passion. —Resurrec-

tion: see Resurrection. —model for living: 133. see also: Imitation of Jesus Christ. —judge: 19, 45. —and souls: see Soul. —and the Company: see Company. —and the Church: 70. see also: the Church. —and the poor: 45, 75, 155. see also: the Poor, Service of the Poor, Gentleness, Charity, Humility.

JOAN of CUSA, St.: 181.

JOHN THE BAPTIST, St.: 35.

JOSEPH, St.: 47.

JOY —with God: 10, 41, 203, 207. —in suffering: see Illness, Suffering. —in the service of the poor: see Service of the poor. —of Louise de Marillac: 19.

JUDGMENT —of God: 19, 34. —of others: prudence and discernment: 131, 152, 177.

JUSTICE —of God: 8, 17, 18, 194, 207. —hunger and thirst for: 72.

KEY of the Motherhouse: 112, 181.

KINGDOM of Heaven —meditation of Louise de Marillac: 175.

KNOWLEDGE of the human person by Louise de Marillac: see Psychology. —of the sisters by Louise de Marillac: 160. —of self: 153, 206.

LADIES OF CHARITY: 155, 156. see also: Meetings, Confraternity.

LA FÈRE —catechism: 216.

LAUNDRESS —her duties: 89.

LAUNDRY —Motherhouse: 100.

LAWSUITS —do not provoke them: 67.

LEAVING the Company; the causes: 218.

LEGRAS, Mlle. Louise: see de Marillac, Louise.

LE MANS —Missioning of sisters: 119.

LENT —meditation of Louise de Marillac: 22.

LEPINTRE, Jeanne D.C. —sent to LeMans: 119.

LETTERS —to be written every two weeks: 135. —to be given to the Superioress: 79. —various: 104.

LYING: 169.

LIFESTYLE: 109. see also: Simplicity.

LIGHT received by Louise de Marillac: 3, 4.

LINEN: 30, 31, 52, 56.

LIVESTOCK of the Confraternities: 51, 53, 55.

LIVING QUARTERS of Louise de Marillac: 39.

LOVE —of God: 11, 17, 19, 20, 21, 33, 34, 38, 43, 45, 72, 94, 136, 152, 173, 184, 197, 198, 200, 201; meditation of Louise de Marillac on: 209. —of the poor: see Char-

ity, Service of the Poor. —among sisters: see Affection, Charity, Cordiality. —of enemies: 20. —of vocation: 162.

LOYALTY: 104, 105.

LUCIFER: 11. see also: Devil.

LULLEN, Marie D.C. —sent on mission: 129.

MAGI: 75.

MAN —creation: 73, 199, 207. —his freedom: 149, 171, 195. —his greatness: 139, 199, 201, 208. —loved by God: 148, 171, 172, 174. —pilgrim on earth: 139. —Perfect Man, Jesus Christ: 195. —comportment with men: 119, 206. see also: Prudence.

MANAGEMENT: see Goods.

MARIE, D.C. —Saint-Denis: her death: 121.

MARILLAC, Louise de —biography: see Birth, Marriage, Widowhood, Living Quarters. —spirituality: see Rule of Life, Holy Spirit, Incarnation, Divine Providence, Trinity, Gift of self to God, Darkness of soul. —qualities: see Humility, Humor, Joy, Perceptiveness, Tenderness, Trials, Complaints. —Foundress of the Company: see Superioress General. —relationship with the sisters: see Attention, Tact, Travel. —relationship with the poor: see the Poor, Service of the poor.

MARRIAGE of Louise de Marillac: 27. —of Mary: 13, 193.

242

MARTHA, St.: 181.

MARTYROLOGY —reading of: 77, 187.

MARY —in the foreknowledge of God: 74. —chosen by God: 172. —Immaculate Conception: 73, 213. see also: Immaculate Conception. —birth: 13. —Mother of God: 5, 13, 14, 38, 135, 150, 173. see also: Incarnation. —Jesus in her womb: 71, 173, 216. —Nativity of Jesus: 24. see also: Nativity. —Nazareth: see Nazareth. —marriage: 13, 193. —awaiting the coming of the Holy Spirit: 26, 124, 198. —full of grace: 136, 214, 220. —Light of the World: 74. —Mother of Mercy: 136. —Mediatrix: 13, 150, 213. —Co-Redemptrix: 215. —and the Trinity: 215. —and the Eucharist: 202, 203. —and the Redemption: 34. —her virtues: 47, 135, 193. see also: Gentleness, Humility. —imitation of Mary: 47, 134. —prayer to Mary: 5, 6, 16, 74, 151. —prayers of Louise de Marillac: 13, 135. —Mother of the Company: 74, 221. —Patroness of the Daughters of Charity: 63. —Consecration to Mary: see Oblation. —Office of the Blessed Virgin: 5.

MASS —what it is: see Eucharist. —daily: 5, 90. —during trips: 69. —for the Confraternities: 51, 54.

MASTERS —the poor are our masters: 146.

MATERNITY of Mary: 5, 13, 216.

MEALS of the sick: 32, 88, 90, 91, 95.

MEAT for the sick: 28, 32, 90, 95.

MEDITATION: 4, 61, 75, 89, 129. —throughout the day: 207. —during journeys: 68.

MEETINGS of the Ladies of Charity: 66, 156. —of the sisters: see Conferences.

MEMBER of Jesus Christ: see the Poor.

MERCY OF GOD: 9, 11, 19, 34, 136, 207.

MIDY, Jacquette D.C. —her death: 121.

MISSIONING of sisters to Montreuil: 129. —of other sisters: 119, 159.

MISUNDERSTANDING among sisters: 153. see also: Discord.

MOCKERY: 23.

MODERATION: 69, 87, 106, 182. see also: Simplicity in lifestyle.

MODESTY: 68, 93, 105, 109, 111, 178.

MONEY —for the poor: 82, 134. —see also: Goods, Allowances. —the dangers of handling: 166, 205. —of the Confraternities: 29, 31, 50, 55.

MONTREUIL-SUR-MER —Missioning of sisters: 129.

243

MOREAU, Marguerite D.C. —sent to Poland: 159.

MORTIFICATION: 7, 26, 143, 166, 192. —corporal: see Hair Shirt. —thoughts of Louise de Marillac: 166.

MOSES: 136.

MOTHERHOUSE of the Daughters of Charity. —duties of: see Assistant, Cook, Procuratrix, Portress. see also: Offices. —regulation: 77, 101, 120. —fall of the ceiling: see Fall. —reception: see Reception.

MULTIPLICATION of the loaves: meditation of Louise de Marillac: 140.

MURMURS: 121, 161, 168. —accepting them as Christ did: 184.

MUSTARD SEED —meditation of Louise de Marillac: 175.

NANTES —arrivals and departures of the sisters: 170.

NANTEUIL-LE-HAUDOIN —establishment: 70.

NATIVITY —of Jesus: 24, 45, 135. see also: Christmas, Incarnation. —of Mary: 193.

NAZARETH: 40, 47.

NEEDS of the poor. —knowing them: 134, 157. —discovering new needs: 158.

NEUFVILLE-ROY —visit of the Confraternity by Louise de Marillac: 51, 54.

NIGHT DUTY —sister charged with it in the hospitals: 89, 92, 96.

OBEDIENCE: 4, 27, 155, 173, 190. —thoughts of Louise de Marillac: 144. —The Vow: 75. —to God: 35, 43. see also: Will of God. —to the Administrators: 131, 133. —to the confessors of the poor: 82. —to the doctor: 82, 116. —to the Officers: 103, 105. —to Priests of the Mission: 119. —to the Rule: see Rule. —to the Sister Servant: 155. —to the Superiors: 133. —of Jesus Christ: 12, 41, 47. —of Mary: 193.

OBLATION —of Louise de Marillac to God: 40-44, 195, 196, 197. to Mary: 13.

OFFENDING GOD: see Sin.

OFFICERS —functions: 78, 101-119. see also: Assistant, Procuratrix, Treasurer. —of the Confraternities of Charity: 33, 66.

OPENNESS of heart, for communication with the Superiors: 106.

ORDER of the day of the Daughters of Charity: 61.

ORGANIZATION in the hospital: 89, 95, 162.

ORIGINS —the Daughters of Charity must live according to their poor origins: 160, 165, 205, 216, 218. —they must not live as do the Ladies of Charity: 166, 217.

OVERABUNDANCE —to be avoided: 182.

244

PARADISE: 137, 138, 179.

PARISH —girls of: 63, 65. —regulation: 82.

PASCHAL MYSTERY: 49. see also: Death of Jesus Christ, Resurrection.

PASSION of Christ: 22. see also: Redemption, Cross.

PASSIONS —combatting them: 143, 166.

PATIENCE in times of difficulty: 132, 192. —toward the Administrators: see Respect. —toward the poor: see Gentleness.

PAUL, St. —apostle: 9, 137.

PEACE —live in: 26. with God: 203. with the sisters: see Forbearance. in imitation of Mary: 13.

PEASANTS —helped by the Charities: 51, 54. —priority to be given them: 218.

PENANCE: 7, 122. —Sacrament: 194.

PENTECOST —feast: 122. —fall of the ceiling: 122.

PERCEPTIVENESS of Louise de Marillac with regard to the Company: 216-218.

PERSECUTION —bearing with it: see Accusations.

PERSEVERANCE: 143, 221.

PETER, St.: 27.

PHARMACIST —her duties: 98, 99, 114, 185.

PILGRIMAGE —meditation of Louise de Marillac: 139.

PLACEMENT —of poor girls: 98. —of foundlings: 80. see also: Foundlings.

PLAN OF GOD —for souls: 35, 195, 201. see also: Creation. —for the Company: 43, 122, 152. see also: Company, Service of the poor, Vocation. —for the Virgin Mary: 13, 193. see also: Mary. —for Louise de Marillac: 26, 40.

POLAND —second missioning of sisters: 159.

PONT SAINTE-MAXENCE —visit of the Confraternity by Louise de Marillac: 50, 53.

POOR, The —members of Jesus Christ: 199, 201, 218. —our masters: see Masters. —first served: 180. see also: Service of the poor, Community Sharing. —those who must serve the Company: 50, 53, 66, 217. —working for: 4. —see also Foundlings, Galley Slaves, the Sick, Service of the poor.

PORTAIL, Antoine C.M. —Paris: 119.

PORTRESS —her duties: 100, 110, 179.

POVERTY: 4. —visible poverty of the sisters: see Money, Allowances, Community Sharing. —of the Company: 205, 218. —of

Louise de Marillac: 27. —maintaining the poverty of their origins: see Origins. —The Vow: 75.

PRAISE of God: see Thanksgiving, Prayer.

PRAYER: 61, 62, 133. see also: Meditation. —formation to: 108. —ejaculatory prayers: 6, 208. —preparation for: see Preparation. —repetition of: see Repetition of prayer. —of the children: 75. —of Louise de Marillac: 7, 11. —for the daily offering: 125. —at Communion: 219. —to the Holy Spirit: 196, 197. 219. —to Mary: 13, 135. —to the Trinity: 125.

PREPARATION —for death: 44, 97, 121, 123. —for prayer: 187.

PRESCRIPTIONS of the doctors: 61. see also: Obedience to the doctor.

PRESENCE OF GOD: 6, 105, 216. —real presence in the Eucharist: 203, 216.

PRIDE: 22, 40, 168. —thoughts of Louise de Marillac: 168.

PRIESTHOOD: 57.

PRIESTS —the respect due them: 134.

PROCURATOR: 29, 56.

PROCURATRIX —her duties: 106. —elected procuratrix: see Gressier.

PRUDENCE: 68, 182. —in words: 114, 116, 131, 132. —in comportment: 68, 119, 134, 205. —necessary for Superiors: 102-104.

PSALMS: 199.

PSYCHOLOGY of Louise de Marillac: 97.

PUNISHMENT of the children: 188.

PURGATORY: 71, 179.

PURITY: 25. —for the Company: 71. —for the children: 188. —of Mary: 71, 151. —of intention: 45, 132. see also: Simplicity.

READING —learning to read: 61. —spiritual: 4, 5, 6, 62, 77, 129.

RECEPTION —of the sick: 85, 96. —at the Motherhouse by the Sister Portress: 110. —of the sisters: 170, 179, 191. see also: Schoolgirls.

RECOLLECTION: 43, 105, 138. see also: Prayer, Presence of God, Silence.

RECONCILIATION: see Confession, Forgiveness. —of human nature with God: 38. see also: Redemption.

RECREATION: 62, 91, 175.

REDEMPTION: 7, 15, 16, 17, 18, 20, 23, 34, 40, 73, 142, 145, 163, 175, 199, 213, 218. —meditation of Louise de Marillac: 149. see also: Death of Christ.

246

REGISTER of the receipts and expenditures: 64, 97, 106. —of the admissions and discharges of the sick: 100.

REGULATIONS —observe them: 155. —Order of the day: 61, 77. —of the Motherhouse: 101, 120. —for the sisters of the hospitals: 84, 89. —for the sisters working with children: 75, 80, 188. —for the sisters working with galley slaves: 83. —for the sisters of the Hôtel-Dieu: 81. —for the sisters of the parishes: 82. —for the sisters of the villages: 85. —for the sisters going to LeMans: 119. —see also: Rules. —Regulation of the Confraternities: 30. —of the life of Louise de Marillac: 4, 10.

RELIGIOUS —do not visit with them too often: 81, 93.

REMEDIES: 86, 114. —for the sisters: see Care of the sick.

RENT for the sisters' house. —Chantilly: 165.

REPETITION OF PRAYER: 61, 77, 79, 112, 187.

REPORT —of a regular visitation: 160. —of a Confraternity meeting: 66.

REQUEST OF FORGIVENESS: 109, 131.

RESOLUTIONS —of a retreat: 207. —of Louise de Marillac: 4, 11.

RESPECT —toward the Administrators: 119, 132; the Ladies of Charity: 82, 155, 206; the doctors: 82; the young girls: 119; the poor: 82; the priests: 82, 134; the sisters: 177; everyone: 131. —respect for the tasks of others: 85. —human respect: 143.

RESPONSIBILITY in the Community: see Assistant, Officers, Sister Servant, Superioress General.

RESURRECTION: 23, 49, 70.

RETREAT —of Louise de Marillac: 7; her thoughts: 17, 24, 36, 39, 44, 146.

ROOM for the sick to await care at the Motherhouse: 111. —of the hospitals: 216.

ROSARY: 6, 91, 92, 108, 190. —with nine beads: 71.

RULES of the Daughters of Charity. —observe them; with fidelity and exactitude: 102, 117, 165, 205, 206. —in the service of the poor: see Service of the poor. —explanation to the young sisters: 109. —comments of Louise de Marillac: 186.

SACRAMENTS —preparation of the sick for their reception: 82, 84. —are received too late by the sick: 49, 53. —formation of the sisters: 109. —reception in church: 15. —Sacrament of Reconciliation: see Confession. —see Baptism, Communion, Extreme Unction.

SAINT-CLOUD —visit of the Confraternity: 27.

248

SISTER SERVANT —choice of: 162. —her functions, her duties: 88, 160. —and her Assistant: 88. see also: Cordiality, Gentleness, Forbearance, Tenderness. —what is owed her by her companions: 177.

SISTERS —older sisters: respect them: 109. —young sisters: 108. —sick sisters: 115; their care: see Care. —sisters working with children: see Foundlings; in the parish: see Parish, Village; in the hospitals: see Hospital; with galley slaves: see Galley Slaves.

SLANDER —bear with it: 191.

SOULS: 171, 173, 174. see also: Man. —redeemed by the blood of the Son of God: 8, 14, 220. —in Purgatory: 7, 79.

SPIRIT —of the Company of the Daughters of Charity: 162. —of faith toward Superiors: 177. —spirit of secretiveness: meditation of Louise de Marillac: 168.

SPIRITUAL CHARITY: 105, 130. see also: Warnings.

SPIRITUAL LIFE —what it is: 197-199. see Meditation, Prayer, God, Jesus Christ. —in the Confraternities: 31, 50-56.

SPIRITUAL TESTAMENT of Louise de Marillac: 221.

SUBMISSION: 155. see also: Obedience, Community Life, Will of God.

SUFFERINGS —accepting them as did Christ: 56, 137, 184. —meditation of Louise de Marillac: 137. —accepting them in the service of the poor: 131. —of Christ: 22-24. —in Purgatory: 71. —of Louise de Marillac for her sins: 8, 9, 34-36.

SUPERIOR GENERAL: 63, 64.

SUPERIORESS GENERAL: 63-65, 102. —Louise de Marillac wishes another to take her place: 139.

SUPERIORS —attitude toward them: see Obedience, Respect, Sister Servant.

SUSPICION of sisters: see Accusations.

TACT of Louise de Marillac. —toward the poor: 87. see also: Cordiality, Gentleness, Service of the poor. —among the sisters: 130. see also: Cordiality, Respect, Forbearance.

TEMPTATION: 43. —against one's vocation: 205.

THANKSGIVING to God: 208; for one's vocation: 124; for the Eucharist: 202-204.

THIEF —The Good Thief and the Bad Thief: 22.

THIRST —need of nature: 72. —of Christ: 22, 23, 24. —for justice: 72.

TIME —waste of: 98, 111.

TRADES for the Hospice of the Name of Jesus: 163, 164.

TRANQUILITY of the soul: 25.

TRANSFIGURATION: 74.

TRAVEL —conduct of sisters during trips: 68, 69, 129. —of Louise de Marillac; —Asnières, Saint-Cloud: 27. —of the sisters; —Nantes: 170. —LeMans: 119. —expenses: 135.

TREASURER of the Confraternities: 28, 52, 54. —of the Company: 78, 106.

TRINITY: 12, 14, 15, 33, 75, 144, 198, 199, 200, 211. —and the Cross: 23. —and the Eucharist: 202-204. —and Mary: 14, 193, 215. —model of union in the Community: 15, 99, 123, 130, 176. —meditation of Louise de Marillac on the Feast of the Blessed Trinity: 73. —her prayer: 125.

TRUST —in God: 21, 42, 156, 194, 203, 208; the example of Mary: 193. —of the sisters toward the Superiors: 103, 119. see also: Divine Providence.

TRUTH —of God: 20-22. —it is humility: 20.

UNION —with God: 56, 72, 94, 141, 198, 208; of Louise de Marillac: 27, 219. —with the Church: 71. —with the poor: 71. —among sisters: 99, 123, 130, 153, 176, 177, 221. —necessary for the service of the poor: 154.

VANITY: 201.

VEIL of the Daughters of Charity: 68.

VERNEUIL —visit of the Confraternity by Louise de Marillac: 49, 52.

VILLAGE —Regulation for the sisters: 85. —origin of the sisters: 63-65, 216.

VINCENT DE PAUL —and the Company of the Daughters of Charity: see Company, Conferences, Superior General. —and the Confraternities of Charity: 156. see also: Meetings, Confraternity.

VINEGAR: 118. —precaution against contagion: 90.

VIRGIN MARY: see Mary.

VIRGINITY of Mary: 5, 13.

VIRTUE: see Perfection. —of their state: see Spirit of the Daughters of Charity.

VISIT of the sick poor: 61, 218. —in their homes: 65. —of the sick in the Confraternities: 49, 50, 52, 53, 54, 55. —of the surgeon-doctor: 99. —visit of the Confraternities by Louise de Marillac: 27, 28, 49, 52, 65.

VOCATION of the Daughter of Charity. —its greatness: 120, 123, 159. —loving and esteeming it: 143, 162, 205, 206. —vocation of Louise de Marillac: 40-44, 48.

VOWS —of Louise de Marillac: 9, 11. —of Mary: 193. —The Formula of the Vows: 146.

WARNINGS — manner of giving them: 192; of accepting them: 118, 121, 130. — who must give them: 79; the Sister Servant: 160; the Officers: 105; the sisters among themselves: 130.

WASHING: 86, 119. — of the Apostles' feet by Our Lord: 48. — of the sisters' feet after a journey: 171.

WAY OF THE CROSS: 22.

WIDOWHOOD of Louise de Marillac: 12, 13.

WIDOWS in the Company of the Daughters of Charity: 63-65.

WILL OF GOD — fulfilling it: 4, 12, 22, 37, 43, 47, 154, 184, 208.

WINE for the sick: 32, 67, 92, 95.

WISDOM OF GOD: 21, 200.

WITNESS: 200, 201.

WOMAN — her greatness: 156. — of the Gospel: 63. — devout: 6. — pregnant: 116.

WORD OF GOD — Perfect Man: 195. see also: Incarnation.

WORDS of Jesus on the Cross: 22-24, 206.

WORK: 86. — with love and ardor: 116, 117, 176. — necessary for the Daughters of Charity: 83; accomplish all tasks: 100; asking what is needed: 83. — in order to earn one's living: 166. — for the elderly of the Hospice of the Name of Jesus: 163.

WORKS OF GOD — their continuation: see Plan of God.

WORLD — break with: see Detachment.

YOUNG GIRLS — reception: 86. see also: Schoolgirls.

YOUNG SISTERS — formation: 108. — duties toward older sisters: 109.

ZEAL: 192.

ROAN   **ROCHELLE**   **BORDEAUX**   **CALIS**

THE QVENNE

GE. MAN

MAR WIFFE

CONT. MAN

LAYERS WIFFE

An Explication of the
Archbishoprikes
Bishoprikes
Colges
Parlement Cite

THE PARTS OF MEDITERRANE SEA